WHAT STUDENTS LEARNED IN GYM CLASS

A Qualitative Study
of Required Physical Education

WHAT STUDENTS LEARNED IN GYM CLASS

A Qualitative Study of Required Physical Education

Virginia S. Cowen

With a Preface by
Teresa Kay-Aba Kennedy

The Edwin Mellen Press
Lewiston•Queenston•Lampeter

Library of Congress Cataloging-in-Publication Data

Cowen, Virginia S.
  What students learned in gym class : a qualitative study of required physical education /
Virginia S. Cowen ; with a Preface by Teresa Kay-Aba Kennedy.
     p. cm.
  Includes bibliographical references and index.
  ISBN-13: 978-0-7734-3744-9
  ISBN-10: 0-7734-3744-4
  1. Physical education and training--United States--Evaluation. I. Title.
  GV362.C68 2009
  613.7071--dc22

                          2009052069

hors série.

A CIP catalog record for this book is available from the British Library.

        The Edwin Mellen Press   The Edwin Mellen Press
              Box 450   Box 67
         Lewiston, New York   Queenston, Ontario
         USA 14092-0450   CANADA L0S 1L0

                      The Edwin Mellen Press, Ltd.
                      Lampeter, Ceredigion, Wales
                      UNITED KINGDOM SA48 8LT

                  Printed in the United States of America

To Kate, Sissy, and TC

Table of Contents

Preface

This book comes at an important time as we battle this nation's health crisis. As a qualitative inquiry into physical education from elementary through high school, it tells stories of men and women who did not learn about exercise in gym class. In a systematic way, Dr. Virginia Cowen offers a delightful read with funny and insightful stories of real experiences that uncover some of the gaps in physical education in the U.S. For example, some who were interviewed felt marginalized and tried to avoid gym at all cost, even if they were high achievers in other subjects. One man was put in remedial gym class simply because he wasn't coordinated. Others showed up to class, but didn't get a chance to participate because they were not naturally inclined to excel in team sports. One woman recalled learning how to play poker during gym since she wasn't chosen to play basketball. Some were even bullied – sometimes by the teacher – because of seemingly inadequate physical skills. For many, gym even became a deterrent to future involvement in certain forms of activity. Most of the stories reinforced the important role of trained and sensitive gym teachers who respect and teach all children to the extent of their capabilities.

Personally, I don't remember gym class – only running around in third grade playing games. It was where I got my first set of stitches. Everything else about gym is a blur. Reading this book, I now understand that I was one of the lucky ones since I was athletic. My love of fitness came from my family. I started dance lessons at three years old and yoga with my mom at four. When I was five years old, I ran the "Gal's Club." It was an exercise club that consisted of three members: Mom, my sister and me. I had already developed an attitude toward health. In my early years, I had been put in situations and classes where I was taught *how* to do healthy activities. At the YMCA, I was on the swimming and gymnastics teams, and then later in high school, I ran track and learned how to

fence. By the time I joined the intramural crew team at Wellesley College, it was a continuation of the fitness habits I'd developed during my life. As a corporate executive, I continued with aerobics and later trained professionally in fitness, holistic health, and yoga. Now, my career is focused on helping people live healthy, productive and empowered lives.

Having lead many community-based health programs, I've come to realize that it is not enough for us to tell people what to do. *We must actively show them how to be well and fit.* This book makes it clear that we have failed in this respect, and it highlights the need to reform physical education. The research in the book reveals that adults tend to participate in lifestyle-related physical activity such as practicing yoga, strength training, and doing cardio like cycling or aerobics. Why aren't children being taught these activities in school? Wellness coaches and yoga teachers, like me, often pick up where gym teachers have dropped the ball. We teach adults how to exercise and take care of their wellbeing because they did not learn these skills in gym class. Physical education can play an important role in combating the growing epidemic of childhood obesity. When movement is promoted as a positive experience, it can boost self-esteem and self-efficacy fostering a life-long relationship with fitness. What if my parents had not put me in ballet and Tiny Tots? With my unmemorable gym experiences, my love of fitness and future career may have been sidelined.

Physical education requirements are either non-existent or inadequate in many states. In reading the stories in this book, it is clear that we need to improve both quantity (the number of hours of gym) and quality (the training of the teacher and structure of the curriculum). National organizations, like the American Heart Association, are advocating minimum standards for student learning in physical education to improve the health of the next generation. Gym class is not supposed to be a diversion from academic studies. Rather, as Dr. Cowen points out, it can be a vital opportunity to impart instruction on exercise, physical fitness, and health. In this way, some adults won't have to suppress gym class memories and

feel they need to be re-educated later in life. We will all be "the lucky ones," equipped with the skills to live healthy, productive and active lives.

Teresa Kay-Aba Kennedy, PhD is President of Power Living Enterprises, in New York City and the founder of the first yoga studio in Harlem. She is the author of the *40 Days to Power Living: Think, Eat & Live on Purpose* and *The Power Living Pledge: An Affirmation for a Purposeful & Powerful Life.* Dr. Kennedy is a national spokesperson for the American Heart Association and a member of the Board of Directors for Yoga Alliance.

Acknowledgements

I am thankful to all who were willing to share stories about their gym class experiences. The seeds of this project were planted at Arizona State University and Mesa Community College. The research, interviews, transcriptions, and writing were completed at Queensborough Community College, the City University of New York. The Professional Staff Congress of the City University of New York (PSC-CUNY) provided partial funding for this project. I am grateful to the members of the Popular Culture Association/American Culture Association for providing the opportunity for me to present the beginnings of the book at the PCA/ACA Conference in New Orleans. This project would not have happened without Jennie O. Fisher who heroically and tirelessly transcribed hours of interview tapes. I am indebted to Kelly Lang for her interest in and enthusiasm about this topic. Finally, the personal encouragement and support I received from Fred, Katherine, Theresa, Stephanie, Felix, and Madeleine helped me to make the idea for this book into a reality.

Introduction

I failed gym in high school. Not entirely, just the last quarter of tenth grade. Luckily our quarter grades were averaged so I passed for the semester. But still I failed. It was the first time I ever received an F on a report card. Strangely, that quarter was the last time I was ever required to enroll in standard gym class. After that semester, exercise would be by my own choice forever.

My earliest memory of gym class is chasing a ball around for about an hour every week or so in the school parking lot or church basement. At my Midwestern parochial elementary school, gym, music, and art were occasional events. They were treats. Every so often we would be released from our academic classes to do something creative or physical. In elementary school it never occurred to me that gym class had a purpose.

By middle and high school, gym was different. It was no longer running around and having fun. We played team sports. This required skill and knowledge of the rules. We were usually expected to know the rules. I had never really learned the rules so it was hard for me to remember what to do. Mostly we played kickball, softball, basketball, volleyball. I remember the balls. Every one of them hit me in the face at one time or another. I know the balls were not at fault, it was my lack of skill at catching or dodging out of the way. I really wanted to learn to play sports. It looked like fun. But I did not feel like I belonged in gym class.

Gym reinforced what I already knew: I was not skilled at sports. Since I lacked skill and did not know the rules, I often sat on the sidelines while other girls played. The girls who were good at sportsand knew the rulesgot to pick the teams, players, and positions. If I did get to play, I stood in the back or in the outfield. Often I sat in the bleachers watching and waiting for class to be over. Unskilled athletes like me were best put out of the way where we could not interfere with the game. It went on around us and without us. The only thing

everyone got to usually participate in was the calisthenics warm up and occasional individual activity. I do not remember learning much about fitness.

When I arrived at college, the first class I signed up for was modern dance. I had always wanted to take dance lessons. I never got to dance in gym. My modern dance teacher was a graduate student from Israel. She was beautiful, stern, and graceful. She ran the dance warm up like a boot camp. Everyone was expected to participate to the best of his or her ability, no exceptions.

When students could not master a movement she worked with them; tirelessly demonstrating, encouraging, and reinforcing. It was my first positive experience in group-oriented exercise. I learned to turn, leap, lunge, roll, and memorize dance combinations. I was not a very good dancer but it did not matter. I learned that it did not have to be beautiful or perfect. Participating was important. Even though I sucked I still had a place in class. Unlike gym class, I belonged. I signed up for more dance classes in college.

As an adult, I finally learned to exercise. I enrolled in a class to learn to run. I went on to finish several marathons. I ride my bicycle, practice yoga, and do Pilates. I walk, hike, and sometimes lift weights. I exercise regularly but I rarely throw, catch, or hit a ball. That still inspires fear. None of my adult physical activity resembles gym class. There are few rules and usually no teams. It is about having fun. Exercise as an adult is different. I only have to depend on me.

Interested in fitness, I pursued training, took workshops, earned certifications, and eventually started teaching people to exercise. I went to graduate school to study exercise science and behavior. Along the way I met men and women who wanted to become fit but did not know what to do. I met people from the bleachers and outfield who—like me—had never learned to exercise in gym class. Things seemed to balance out—sort of.

One memorable day in graduate school I listened to my classmates extol the virtues of gym class. They said that gym class in elementary, middle, and high school taught teamwork, healthy habits, encouraged positive self-perception, and

promoted self-esteem. My classmates intoned that gym class prepared students for lifetime participation in exercise and physical activity. I honestly thought they were joking. Shocked at what they were saying, I could not contain myself. I told them that gym class for me caused bad physical self-perception and contributed to poor self-esteem because of the focus on sports-based skills. For me gym was about marginalization, favoritism, and bullying. I told them that I had never really learned much in gym class. They told me I was wrong. As I sat there I realized that they were all the jocks. I was the lone outfielder and bleacher dweller in the classroom that day. They would have been the ones who got to play in gym. They would not have noticed classmates like me on the sidelines. They really did not know.

The year that I failed gym was the only time I remember receiving points for actually doing anything: winning a tournament. I won a badminton tournament. More correctly I participated in winning a badminton tournament. My doubles partner in badminton was on the tennis team so she had a way with a racquet. My contribution in our doubles matches was to stand on the court holding my racquet and do my best to stay out of her way while she hit the shuttlecock. She was really good. I have a vague memory of hitting something back over the net at a very surprised opponent. Mostly I was decorative. Winning the tournament was worth twenty points. In gym class currency it was the equivalent of one powder-blue gym suit, a pair of socks, and sneakers: Every semester I religiously counted up my points for gym. I suspected that the gym teacher never awarded me the points for the tournament. That is the only reason I can think of to explain why I failed. She probably forgot because it was barely conceivable that someone like me could ever win anything in gym class.

Attitudes and enjoyment of gym class are influenced by a variety of factors including the teacher, the curriculum, the school environment, and the

student's own motivation.[1] All students should have a place in gym class. Gym should be enjoyable so that all students can learn something about how to be active, why exercise is important for good health, and how they can do this on their own. That was not my gym experience. I learned about exercise and physical activity in spite of gym.

I knew that there were others who had spent gym class in the outfield or bleachers. Maybe we all had "not learned" the same sorts of things. I began to recognize that there were others like me who did not learn in gym. I met them occasionally. Men who came to the health club where I worked would only try to lift the heaviest weights. They did not know how or why to use the cardiovascular equipment. I met women who would ask me about lifting weights "for the bone density thing." Many of them thought that free weights were dangerous.

Curious about these people, and reflecting on my experience, I began to collect stories. I wanted to know how other people remembered gym class and how it related to their exercise habits as adults. Initially I sought a convenience sample of people who had interesting stories or memories about gym. More people were referred to me when they heard about the project. All of the subjects in this project agreed to participate in a series of interviews. The names and identifying information for the subjects in this book have been changed to maintain their confidentiality.

For some people gym class was no more or less of a memory than academic classes at the same age. Most people played team sports in gym; very few play team sports regularly as adults. Nearly everyone I spoke with was confused about how gym class related to lifestyle physical activity. Gym did not help most of them learn how to exercise or be fit. It was comforting to find out that I am not the only person who is afraid of balls.

---

[1] In a two-part analysis of research on physical education, Amade-Escot and Amans-Passaga reviewed curriculum, learning and teacher education. They noted the perception of quality education is different based on gender, cultural, socioeconomic status, skill-level, and physical ability. See also Williams and Germain.

Chapter 1

Skills and Curriculum:

Surviving the Sports-based Overt Gym Curriculum and the Subtle Messages of the Covert Curriculum

> I don't have the best eye-hand coordination and so anything involving hitting a ball is something I try to avoid.

The purposes of non-academic courses in elementary, middle, and high school center around the concept of "whole-person" education. Theoretically this enables schools to produce smart children who can excel on standardized tests, but who will also be happy and healthy members of society.[2] Gym class initially aimed to prepare young men for war. When this was no longer a societal need, physical education remained a part of the curriculum and was offered to both boys and girls. The goal of gym class shifted to helping students develop motor skills and eventually to educate students on physical activity and a healthy lifestyle. This paradigm shift has slowly occurred over the past fifty to sixty years.

At all ages, students in gym are now expected to learn how to be physically active.[3] They are also expected to learn about the benefits of exercise and physical activity, i.e. why they should be physically active. Children in kindergarten and the early primary grades are expected to learn how to move and how to behave properly in gym class. This is accomplished by teaching them how

---

[2] For example see Standard 2.2 New Jersey's in Comprehensive Health Education and Physical Education Curriculum Framework outlining life skills along with personal and interpersonal skills that are applicable to activities in gym class.

[3] Bailey notes that gym and sports participation has potential to favorably impact health. This review also suggests that the benefits and outcomes expected from physical education are dependent on many factors including the student's qualitative experience in gym.

to take turns, work together, stand in line, follow directions, and participate.[4] While order and discipline are ideas that probably hang over from the military gym days, but are also aspects of teams sports. They are important concepts in gym during the early grades. So is getting kids moving.

For children, movement is important to physical development. Motor skills taught in gym that are used in sports include movements like: running, jumping, hitting, kicking, throwing, catching, pivoting, and blocking. Moving helps bone and muscle growth, eye – hand coordination, and promotes cardiorespiratory fitness. Children can develop physical self-confidence by learning how to move. Gym class is supposed to be fun, but it is not for all students. Kelly recalls:

> Gym was imposed upon us so it was not something that we chose. It was a pretty structured schedule. You went to the gym at the assigned time and you did what you were told to do. It was pretty much: Line up and do it.

Sometimes students are instructed in the components of physical fitness: muscular strength and endurance, flexibility, cardiorespiratory health. Sometimes students are given homework and are expected to participate in regular exercise outside of gym class. More often students are expected to learn how to play sports. Alas, when sports are the primary vehicle used in gym, gym can prove difficult for unskilled students like Kelly.

> I absolutely stink at sports. I cannot make a baseball bat connect with a baseball or softball. I don't care if you throw me a beach ball, I probably couldn't bat it. Basketball? Forget it. So to me, team sports were something where I stunk. I wasn't good enough. Why bother?

The early attempts at adding physical education programs to schools were largely to compensate for the societal shift away from agriculture and labor to sedentary occupations. At the time, experts agreed that physical education must not detract from academic studies and should be able to be executed in

---

[4] See Salmon and Carter. Young children are aware that the gym classroom is managed differently than other classes. Some students perceive the classroom process concepts to be more important than gym content like learning movement or sports skills.

classrooms, without special equipment or specifically-trained teachers. It is probably not surprising that students did not regard in-class exercise as interesting or inspiring. [5]

At one time, playing team sports was considered a logical way to prepare boys for military service. Exercise drills were included in physical education with the aim of improving physical fitness and training students to be obedient.[6] Some gym teachers still seem to adhere to these ideas. It was also fairly easy for a teacher to divide the class in two, throw a ball out on the floor, stand aside and watch what happened. Although the goals of gym were considered to be in common, what constituted gym class was quite different depending on where a student went to school.

Current curricular recommendations for gym state that all students should have the opportunity to be active in an inclusive environment. The challenge in gym class is to provide instruction about exercise and physical activity in a way that imparts knowledge while encouraging socialization and promoting responsibility and individual student accountability. Throwing a ball on the floor would not seem to accomplish much to meet this challenge.

The President's Council on Youth Fitness was established by President Dwight D. Eisenhower in 1956 as a reaction to a report that European children were more physically fit than American children.[7] The goal of the Council was to present the idea that physical fitness should be important to the public. National programs and standards were developed around the goal of getting American kids fit. Adam recalls a calisthenics routine performed to music:

---

[5] In 1926 Williams attributes this phenomena to the lack of facilities and poor physical education teacher training. It calls to mind the possibility that some classrooms might simply moved equipment aside to participate in calisthenics and then return to academic pursuits. This approach would allow time for activity and mimics modern-day recommendations for desk workers to take stretch and movement breaks. While it is realistic, the approach may be no more effective now than it would have been eighty years ago due to the lack of enjoyment.

[6] Discussion of the militaristic approach to gym ranges from Camp to Shephard and Trudeau. Even when the schools are not expected to produce young men fit enough to become soldiers, some gym classes still feature boot camp approaches like unison calisthenics routines.

[7] See http://www.fitness.gov/about_overview.htm for a brief history of the President's Council, now called The President's Council on Physical Fitness and Sports.

I remember Robert Preston (of Music Man fame) telling us to get rid of our chicken fat: "Give that chicken fat back to the chicken and don't be chicken again. No, don't be chicken again."

We'd do sit-ups, jumping jacks, and whatever along with that song. Then I'd get that song in my head and all day long. I couldn't understand why we needed the song to do this. We did this at the beginning of every single gym class before we could do anything fun.

Barbara also remembered the "chicken fat" song from her -Midwestern public school gym class. For her the memory was both disturbing and funny. It did nothing to inspire her in gym.

One of the things they used to do for us in elementary school was play a record called the Chicken Fat Song. We would have to do toe touches, jumping jacks, and things like running in place to warm up for whatever we were going to do. I have never forgotten the song. 'Go you chicken fat, go away. Go you chicken fat, go. It would go on and on and on. It was the stupidest thing. I think it was part of some sort of intentional program like 'run the fat off their little lazy butts' or whatever. It was insane. It was totally nuts. I think they tortured us with the Chicken Fat Song for at least three years. I was a stout child and I actually grew fatter during that time.

What Adam and Barbara are remembering was the Youth Fitness Song, composed by Meredith Wilson in the 1960s. John F. Kennedy embraced Eisenhower's initiative on physical fitness. His administration created an elaborate program that included print and broadcast advertising along with program kits. Part of this kit was "The Chicken Fat Song." Separate versions of the song were recorded for radio play and for school use. The school version led students through a variety of calisthenics.[8]

Did the program motivate generations of students to perform calisthenics ten times every day? Samantha finished a phrase of the song when I sang the first part for her. Susan also remembered starting out gym class in second grade with the same routine. It was a funny, but not an inspiring memory for any of them. The song sounds like a college or high school "fight song." While that might

---

[8] A brief history of this program is outlined on the website for the John F. Kennedy Presidential Library: "The Federal Government Takes on Physical Fitness" www.jfklibrary.org

inspire a team athlete to jump or run or push onward, it did little for non-athletes. It did not inspire them to touch their toes or do jumping jacks daily. Performing calisthenics in unison just felt like a military exercise. At least in the end, the tune was catchy and the song was memorable even if it did not inspire them to slim down.

There are now national, state, and local guidelines for physical education. This involves a patchwork of health policy, education standards, and professional association recommendations that provide the basis for gym curriculum. Basically, gym class is not supposed to be a diversion from academic studies like many students think. Rather it is considered to be a vital opportunity to impart instruction on exercise, physical fitness, and health.

The Centers for Disease Control and Prevention (CDC) recommends 2.5 hours of gym per week for primary school students, and 3.75 hours per week for middle and high school students.[9] That means kids should have gym class most days of the week for at least thirty minutes. Some—but not all—states have time requirements for gym, and some states have recommendations for the course content of gym. Gym class does indeed have a curriculum.

Professional and policy recommendations for gym include having students be physically active during gym class and teaching students about the health benefits of exercise.[10] This is the overt curriculum: what students are expected to learn or master in school. Gym class aims to teach students gross motor skills and fundamental concepts of physical fitnes. Gym class teaches students about physical activity and exercise—and how they are different. Basically physical activity is any type of movement while exercise is planned or purposeful

---

[9] The CDC's Physical Education Curriculum Analysis Tool aims to help educators and administrators evaluate gym programs. This 210-page free handbook outlines recommended content an assessments for different K-12 age groups. Current national standards and a worksheet for possible changes are included along with testimonials from teachers about the publication.
[10] There are a variety of standards for physical fitness and physical activity that are published by different organizations. The National Association for Sport and Physical Education publishes National Standards for Physical Education as well as information about state standards and position papers on gym, activity, and fitness. See: www.aahperd.org/naspe/.

movement.[11] Both physical activity and exercise have an impact on health. Theoretically students who learn how to exercise and why they should might actually engage in exercise on their own. Gym is the only class that has a rationale built into the curriculum. Students are not told why they should learn language skills, science, mathematics, or history. But students are told why they should participate in gym. Physical activity habits established in school years are expected to provide the foundation for lifestyle physical activity. Yet, the vast majority of adults do not exercise on a regular basis. That means that adults who took gym class did not learn what they were supposed to learn.

For gym class to live up to the expectation, it should be relevant, inspiring, and instructional to students who are not athletically inclined as well as the sports-skilled students. Yet much of gym has traditionally centered on team sports. Gym class at Adam's East Coast, suburban, public middle and high school was sports focused. The classes offered an opportunity to learn a little bit about a lot of different sports.

> There was no instruction that I recall about healthy lifestyles or any way to monitor one's health. There was nothing like that. Gym was all about learning a little bit about different sports that you could play. We learned a little bit about basketball, football, or gymnastics, whatever they had equipment for. From there it was more about achievement. I don't ever remember a discussion about things like body mass, weight, heart rate, aerobics, or habits of health. Diet was not mentioned at all. It was more like an exposure to different activities with an emphasis on competition. There was never much instruction.

Adam was exposed to a variety of activities. He was a talented athlete so he often got the opportunity to play and be active in gym. But the gym teachers placed a great deal of emphasis on winning rather than health. They played games by the rules. Darren's gym classes were also sports focused. But at his high school

---

[11] Caspersen, Powell, and Christenson define differences between physical fitness, exercise and overall physical activity. Although the difference between exercise and physical activity is subtle. it can be an important distinction when teaching students or counseling adults about physical fitness and healthy behavior.

there was not much emphasis on either winning or health. They just participated for that period of the day.

> We picked a sport from a list of the —twelve-or-so gym classes that were offered that semester...gymnastics, golf, tennis, hockey, field hockey, basketball, social dance. Things like that. Class would start with a lot of drills. Everyone participated in those and then there would be a game. I do not remember exactly but I think the game would use a regulation number on each side with people subbing in from the sidelines.

Students at his high school had a choice of activities. They could feel a sense of mastery because they focused on one activity for the whole term. Other than social dance, the choices were sports. Lifestyle physical activities, like strength training, fitness walking, or aerobics, were not an option. Darren also recalled that some students sat on the sidelines watching while others played. All students were not given the same opportunity to be active in class.

Clarisse viewed gym as a chore because it was almost entirely focused on team sports that involved balls. She was afraid of balls, so she feared team sports. She was just "never any good at it." She felt that she never learned to exercise as a child because she did not have any skill playing ball. When individual pursuits are included in the curriculum, students often enjoy them, especially students who do not feel that they are competitive. Teaching individual sports like golf, tennis, cycling, weight lifting, archery require special equipment or facilities. Teaching activities like dance, karate, yoga, or Pilates require special training. These are the usual arguments about why these activities are not included in gym class. But activities like these can help students acquire motor skills and learn to exercise. Dance gave Barbara a feeling of self-confidence about movement and about gym.

> We had a huge unit on dance—modern dance. Some teacher in the school was really into it. So she got it into the curriculum. I was not a gifted dancer, but I could do it well. I enjoyed it very much. I was thrilled that we did something that I was good at.

Kelly was neither athletically skilled nor competitive in nature. Line dancing helped her learn about coordination and find meaning in movement.

Sophomore year they made us line up, they turned on some music, and they showed us some steps. Suddenly I realized 'I can do this.' It's not dependent on anyone picking me to be on their team. It's just me moving. When my brain tells my feet, hands, or arms to move, they do what it asks them to do. I'm coordinated, I'm balanced. I can do this. I was accountable only to myself. Given that opportunity I realized that I really could be--not necessarily an athlete--but I could be a moving, living person and not be a loser in gym.

For Jackie, who also felt uncoordinated in gym, learning archery was enlightening.

In high school when we tried archery I was actually pretty good. Of course it helped to imagine I was shooting at someone who got on my nerves. But I could shoot very well. I remember my gym teacher was surprised.

Shooting an arrow requires upper body muscular strength and flexibility, but it does not require the type of coordination required to run and dribble a basketball. During traditional gym activities, Jackie was lost and uninterested. But she was able to feel some success at a non-traditional gym class activity. She did learn a little about physical self-confidence.

Gym class offers the opportunity for behavior and social skillstraining like teamwork, taking turns, and communication. This is good for life skills. Unfortunately it also means that children are not necessarily active in gym class. For young students standing in line, waiting, listening to instructions, and taking turns are perceived as more important aspects of gym class than the actual activities. These learning opportunities are called the covert curriculum. This describes aspects of school that are not content based, but rather are underlying characteristics or concepts that the student learns. Collaboration, conformity, and perseverance are positive aspects of the covert curriculum of school that are relevant to gym class.[12] The objectives of some aspects of the covert curriculum

---

[12] McLoughlan discusses the gap between approaches to teaching and knowledge about effective instructional techniques. Much of school focuses on factual learning. Gym class is different because it is rooted in experience rather than memorization of facts and figures.

can be accomplished by demanding that students play by the rules, work well together, and try hard.

Collaboration is a benefit of team-oriented activities. Members of teams often have specific roles in sports. Success relies on people being willing and able to execute their role. When students of all skill levels are permitted to play, everyone can learn something—even if they do not win the game. They can learn to define tasks or space, and that each team member has a purpose. On a true team everyone belongs.

Conformity in gym class is often accomplished by having students dress in uniforms and engage in simultaneous activities like calisthenics. The Youth Fitness Song is a good example of conformity in gym: synchronized exercise to music. It is rather militaristic, but it does promote discipline. Doing the right thing, at the right time, in the right way teaches students classroom discipline. This might translate to individual discipline if the student is motivated to participate and try to do well gym. Ideally, winning is not as important as effort. But as Adam noted, his gym teachers stressed the importance of winning.

There are a variety of reasons why students may not learn in gym. They may lack skills or not be motivated to try. The feeling of failure is one of the negative outcomes of gym class for many students. Perseverance in sports is essentially encouraging students to continue to try when there is little hope of winning. Part of this is sportsmanship. The basketball team that is losing at halftime is still expected to take the court for the second half of the game. Most of the entrants in a marathon have little chance of winning the race, and yet they run. In gym class, team sports offer good opportunities to teach perseverance. So do skill-oriented activities: like climbing a rope. I met a retired gym teacher who got misty-eyed when she remembered the ropes in her gym. She actually looked back fondly at that activity and she spoke about the importance of caring for the ropes. Thankfully it was not part of gym for me, or maybe I missed that day. For those who did face ropes, it was a memorable activity. Unfortunately it was not often a

good memory. Rope climbing probably was intended to evaluate muscular strength and perhaps perseverance. For Kendra it was just another thing that she could not do well in gym.

> I had to climb a rope. Who the hell knows how to climb a rope? But there were girls that could climb ropes. I was like: how are they climbing a rope? They didn't teach us how to climb a rope. They would just say: 'okay, climb a rope'. I couldn't hang on to the rope without falling."

Barbara was not taught how to climb a rope either. The ropes were an occasional activity that involved no particular instruction. She wonders why it was part of gym at her suburban elementary school since she could not relate the task to any aspect of her life.

> The rope thing only showed up like twice a year. Not like we practiced it or anything. Somehow you were expected to know how to climb up a rope. This is not exactly a skill that one has in everyday life unless you live in a barn. I mean come on! This wasn't a rural school. We weren't getting hay in. It was simply the most bizarre thing. It was probably some standards from the twenties. Back then people did live in barns.

Francis thinks it must have been an activity used to train soldiers and Darren suspects it was just a way to "exhaust the kids." Neither remembers being able to climb to the top. George and Adam were taught how to climb a rope and felt a sense of accomplishment when they were able to reach the top. George remembers that he was 'average' at rope climbing. Adam recalls that he felt more relief than success when he succeeded.

> At first I thought, 'well this is just never going to happen'. I can't do this. I don't want to do this. But when they explained to me that it was more legs than arms and that I didn't have to pull myself up the rope, I was more confident. I remember a great feeling of relief when I got to the top and could actually touch the ceiling.

Perhaps the misty-eyed retired gym teacher was remembering students like George and Adam when she thought of the ropes. They were able to learn and succeed. Perseverance, effort, and success are useful things for students to learn

and feel. For Francis, Darren, Kendra, and Barbara, rope climbing made them feel like failures.

A gym teacher's communication of his/her values and attitudes through words and actions is the hidden curriculum. It is something that lurks beneath the surface yet sets the tone for the whole class. Gender bias, exclusion of unskilled students, or favoritism of athletically-skilled students are often part of the hidden curriculum in gym class.

The usual gender bias in exercise or sports is the message is that girls are not as good as boys. Gender separation can have a legitimate purpose. At my parochial schools, girls and boys always had separate gym classes. I always thought it was a way to preserve our chastity. Segregating gym class by sex does help give girls opportunity to be active, especially when they are less skilled at sports.[13]

Eileen, a talented dancer who was a good athlete, was "often sent to play with the boys because I was good at sports." She learned that gym was about skill and achievement rather than inclusion with her peers. At Miriam's small-town school in the Midwest, the girls and boys had separate gym facilities.

> They boys always got to be in the big the new gym. We were in the old gym. There were two basketball hoops, but no basketballs. We did have a pool table. We had no instruction about how to play pool. We just had the cue and the balls and the pool table and we had to entertain ourselves. I am still a bad pool player. We did sit-ups once in a while. Most of the time we played pool in our regular school clothes. The girls didn't have the things that the boys had and we didn't really learn anything, but as adults we are expected to have learned what the boys learned about exercise.

Exercise and sports for many female adults were affected by Title IX which required gender equality in all aspects of education at institutions that received federal funding of any kind. This federal law, passed in 1972, had a

---

[13] Constantinou, Manson, and Silverman surveyed female students about their attitudes about and perceptions of gym. Even when girls believe that they possess sports skills, they feel that boys have more skill and are more competitive in gym. While this feeds into a common stereotype, the gym teachers noticed that the girls also appeared to enjoy the competitive aspects of gym.

trickle-down effect to K-12 physical education and sports. Essentially, it gave girls opportunities to participate in team sports as well as better gym class opportunities. Unfortunately Miriam graduated from high school before Title IX.

Marty loved basketball and felt like a good player. But his middle school gym teacher also favored the boys with more skill. Marty spent much of gym sitting on the sidelines watching the other boys play. As an adult this still makes him angry. He really wanted to play. Erin also wanted to play. Learning the rules of sports was important in Erin's high school gym class. She dutifully memorized the rules and remembers doing well on written tests. But when it came time to play she also sat on the sidelines watching the more skilled girls play basketball and volleyball.

I remember participating in basketball drills in middle school. Trying to bounce and throw the ball was fun but catching the ball was hard because I was not a good basketball player. We would try to make all kinds of shots. The girls who were on our school basketball team knew exactly what to do and made the most of their shots. I frequently over- or under-shot the basket if I was shooting on the run. Free throws were a bit easier to understand, but I lacked the strength to throw the ball far enough.

The teacher stood on the sidelines watching us do the drills. Sometimes the team captains stood with her. I felt like I was being evaluated for the eventual team draft. When it came time for a game, I usually sat on the sidelines watching the other girls play. If the teacher called me into the game, it was usually towards the end of the class when I could not do much harm to the winning—or losing—team.

What Marty, Erin, and I learned is that we could not participate since we were not as skilled as the other students. We learned that we did not belong on sports teams, even when we were interested in participating. My middle school gym teacher did not seem interested in helping me learn or letting me play. Throughout school, my gym teachers generally kept the skilled girls active and

made kids like me feel that we could never be as successful in team sports as the skilled girls. When I was permitted to try to play, I remember being yelled at by my classmates and sometimes the teacher when I did something wrong. I felt like I got in the way of the game rather than be a part of it. My gym teacher did nothing to dispute that.

George did get help with gym. He admits that he was not athletic, but his school noted that he lacked skill in sports and movement. In middle school he had a rather unusual opportunity to learn in gym class. I had never heard of remedial gym until I talked with George.

> The first day of junior high was one of the worst days of my life. I remember it very distinctly. Without knowing it was going to happen, I was put remedial gym. I didn't even know it existed. They did not test us or anything, but it was obvious I was bad at gym.

> The class was mostly weight lifting. There were four of us that I remember. Two of the other guys and I were very good academically and apparently very poor in gym. And then there was another fellow who had some sort of problem. I don't know if it was a stroke or an aneurysm or something but he needed to rebuild his abilities. He was the only one who had a physical problem that I was aware of. The rest of us were just not competent in gym. But we were perfectly normal, able people.

George was an academic high achiever. For him it was an insult to be put in any remedial course. He called it "spasm" gym. The only thing that made him feel better was that one of his fellow classmates was also academically gifted. He initially felt disgraced by the remedial label. But remedial gym accomplished something for George and his classmates. They made friends and learned how to lift weights. He achieved a more positive physical self-concept and progressed to regular gym class.

Attempts at inclusion in gym for everyone at Franco's high school meant that usually everyone got to play or do something. However, gym at his high school did not help his physical self-concept even though it seemed to include all of the necessary components to help him. The classes included collaborative activities as well as individual and team sports. But it was a hodgepodge of

activities with the skilled athletes "taking gym way too seriously." Franco was somewhat active in gym, but he did not find gym to be meaningful or interesting.

> We usually played a bunch of sports and sometimes did made-up things like adventure camp. That involved trust falls, walking across the floor on sticks while other kids hold them, and things like that. Overall gym was pretty lame. Kids at my school would have loved to learn something like yoga. The girls were always saying that they were going to yoga after school. Why didn't we do yoga in gym? That would have been cool. It would have been worth something.

Franco also received a poor grade for a group choreographed dance and had to perform push-ups when his team lost a volleyball game. He had little instruction in physical fitness.

My graduate school classmates probably got to play in gym. Those of us who did not, or could not, learned other things. Kelly developed social skills; Erin memorized the rules for lots of sports; George became "less pathetic." Climbing a rope can help some a student feel good about themselves—if they succeeded. Although I my middle school gym teacher ignored me, I learned that I mattered in other classes and other activities. I had something to offer at school—it was just not in team sports.

Chapter 2

T.E.A.M.:

The Hazards and Benefits

of Team Sports Activities in Gym

I would love to join in group sports I think. But quite honestly I feel like I can't do that because I was so horrible when I was younger. Team sports were always so fraught with terror.

Sports that are accessible to everyone are an important social and health phenomena.. The key is accessibility. Team sports involve rules, roles, and goals. Good lessons for life, but team sports are not necessarily good for all students. Players must have the skills to play their position and contribute to the group effort. Unfortunately, team sports are not accessible to unskilled students.

When the players lack skill it affects the player and the overall team effort. In a positive situation, this is where students learn about sportsmanship. In a negative situation, the non-skilled student is marginalized. When a student lacks skill, effort and perseverance are important. That should be rewarded. When this does not work, the concepts of teamwork and ideas of sportsmanship fail. Because Barbara lacked the skills to hit or catch a ball, she felt exposed and scared in softball.

One of the worst memories is when I was in 5th gradeevery time I think of it I still feel horrible. We were playing softball in the gym. Everybody had to get up to bat and I never wanted to get up to bat, ever, ever, ever! You know you could sort of take yourself out of the line-up if you're clever and I would do that. Just keep letting somebody go ahead of you in line. There were so many of us, and the teacher wasn't really paying attention and all of us blonde haired girls look alike...

Eventually somebody caught on that I wouldn't bat so they made me get up to bat in front of what seemed like a billion children. The person pitching threw me the ball (the pitcher was in 5th grade and really didn't pitch well) and the ball went wild and I tried to hit it. Of course I missed and they all laughed at me. I broke out in a sweat and I my vision got grainy and it was awful. I wanted to die. My teacher laughed right along with the rest of them.

Good sportsmanship is something that is learned through participation. While this might have been an opportunity for the teacher to discuss sportsmanship and provide encouragement, which is not what happened. It is probably not surprising that Barbara continued to try to avoid participating in softball after that. She would still try to avoid the batting line-up then stand way out in the outfield and pray that the ball would not be hit in her direction. This experience had an impact on her perceptions of teamwork and her physical activity choices as an adult. Barbara is an active adult, but she chooses individual and lifestyle activities rather than team sports.

I have never, ever even remotely considered doing something like the Wednesday night volleyball thing that they have at the Y, because you kind of have to act as a group. I just can't do it even though I love volleyball and it would probably be fun.

I wish that they could have taught me what the point of the group sport was and that they could have made it an atmosphere of acceptable inclusiveness. Then I could have learned how to function within a team in a way that I didn't find threatening. That was one thing I did not learn in gym.

Jackie did not learn about teamwork and sportsmanship in gym either. She was not taught about team interaction even though they played team sports in gym. She wished she had learned more about the rules for sports and team activities, even though she did not have the skill to play. Her gym classes were all girls.

I think teamwork rules prepare you for work situations, especially when working with men. Last week I was at an event and all the honorees were men. In fact I knew a dozen women in that room who would have been

just as qualified for the awards that were being given. The men knew all the rules. They have been functioning in team settings for a long time compared to most women my age.

Gender bias exists in physical education beyond just teamwork. Girls and boys do interact differently in a cooperative setting. Jackie learned about teamwork through other activities like chorus, debate team, and the yearbook committee. In those activities, her teammates were mostly girls but the roles were defined, the work collaborative, and the experience more forgiving than gym class.

Teamwork is an important social and life skill. Aspects from team sports are useful in life and in work-related situations that involve teams. Forming teams involves choosing the people that you want, getting the strong players in the vital roles and the supporting players in other roles. The most important thing is that everybody has the opportunity to play or contribute together using his or her best strengths to achieve the overall goal. Theoretically life/work teams are similar to team sports. However, in these teams most of the participants are not sitting on the sidelines like gym class. Miriam also feels that she missed learning about sportsmanship and teamwork.

> Men can come out of disagreements, shake hands, and be friends. Women my age, who didn't have that sports training, hold it personally. We come out of disagreements or competition and we hold it against each other because we never learned that it's just work or it's just a game.

Team sports were a large part of Kendra's gym experience. But since she was not skilled at sports, she just tried to stay out of the way in gym.

> To this day I don't participate in team things like that. I kind of regret that a good team experience was taken away from me. But I had it in other ways in band and theater. Those became my team experiences. There is something about doing something physical with a group of people and succeeding at it. I don't feel like I had a sense of that in gym.

The concepts of teamwork can be effectively learned through avenues other than team sports. The skills and roles of being on a team are important to

George in his professional life. A top executive in his industry, he works with groups of people all over the world. He did not learn about teamwork playing basketball.

> I didn't mind the idea of basketball. I mean I like watching it but I would panic when I'd get the ball. I'd be fine all the time when I didn't have the ball. I could run around and whatever. I wasn't very aggressive in blocking but I'd would kind of block. But if I got the ball, I didn't know what to do with it, so I would just panic. I would freeze and then I'd try to throw it away to someone. I don't remember any of my teachers trying to tell me what to do with the ball.

> George learned about teamwork in a different sort of activity.

> I was a star on the math team. Maybe not always but math team was a great experience. That was my sports experience. I know it sounds silly. There were about 5 of us I think. We'd have regular practices each week and then we'd go and we'd compete every month in a meet. Then they had a big meet for all the schools in the region so it was like 40 or 50 schools. I think there were like 3 rounds, you'd get certain number of questions and it would be timed. They were very hard math problems. I don't think our team ever won. I did win personally one year as a junior. It was very cool.

Practice, support, consideration, respect, and the opportunity to win or lose were what George learned through math, not sports. Darren also learned about teamwork through math club and in scouting.

> I was a boy scout and we were active. We camped and hiked. Maybe that is a sport, I don't know. In high school I became a senior scout. As a leader, there were definitely times when we'd have to just do something to keep the scouts busy. Let's find some sort of activity to get them to run around and tire themselves out. Let's capture the flag or make something up. Rarely was it a formal team sport. It was more often some aspect that was sort of vaguely scouting-like (whatever that might be.) It was a cooperative rather than a competitive endeavor.

Social sports are sometimes a part of Darren's work life. Usually this involves tennis or golf, but sometimes larger team sports like soccer, football, and volleyball.

> The team sports generally I hate more. Anything that involved eye-hand coordination. I'm more interested in the ability to exercise and to basically

participate as opposed to engaging in a competitive sports activity. I have no interest in golf. I had a golf class in high school which was a complete waste of time. Luckily I have been successful in avoiding business activities that involve golf. I did take tennis in high school and my mother actually arranged for me to take tennis lessons. I got as far as serving, but then I couldn't serve. I just got too frustrated.

For Darren, his frustration with team sports relates primarily to his lack of skill. He works nationally and internationally as part of a team. In his job he has skills and has been successful. But his job does not rely on eye-hand coordination. His job relies on his abilities in other areas. Adam enjoyed participating in team sports, but he does not remember learning that in gym.

I played little league for a while. My father got upset with the coaches. A lot of these guys who were coaching these teams were screamers and yellers. I think my father didn't like me in that atmosphere. As much as he and I both loved baseball and I was good at it, he didn't want me exposed to that kind of environment. But I always enjoyed sports and got involved in sports after school. I was on the soccer team, track team, those sorts of things. I always felt those were the places that I was really doing sports. The stuff I did in gym I just did to get the credit and because I was required to go. I didn't see that as really instructional in any particular way. Gym was simply something that was expected of me in school. I just saw it as an obligation. In gym the kids who were highly skilled dominated the game.

I wish I learned about sports people played that didn't require teams like golf or tennis. I wish I had learned a little bit more about the importance of exercise to my health. There was too much emphasis on sports that require skill rather than sports that basically anybody could play, especially sports where people of smaller dimensions can play and be successful.

Gym involved team activities but not necessarily teamwork. That is a big difference. When it is not teamwork, the structure of a team exists in the form of a group, but there is no cooperative and collaborative effort. The use of team sports

in gym class is a tradition that aims to improve self-esteem, encourage socialization and provide opportunities to improve physical fitness. [14]

Adam did enjoy team participation—outside of gym class. What happened in gym class did not deter Adam from pursuing team activities on an extracurricular basis or as an adult. Adam's transition from team sports to individual activities was a lifestyle choice rather than a conscious effort to avoid team activities as an adult. His favorite activity is cycling, but he did not cycle in gym class.

> I wish I had learned about the variety of sports that I could do for a lifetime rather then everything being so team oriented. I didn't know about a lot of sports that people played that didn't require teams. I played in a men's volleyball league for three years. But then I got my doctorate and I got married. The lifestyle of team sports was really inconvenient. I didn't want to be on somebody else's schedule I didn't want to have to coordinate with a bunch of people. I played some racquetball, I only need one other person for that. But still it required a lot of timing and coordination. I tried golf but I'd have to call weeks in advance for tee times. The bicycle was always at my leisure. It sits there, waits for me, and when I'm ready to go, it's ready to go. I don't have to call anybody up. I don't have to make an appointment. I don't have a bunch of people depending on me showing up.

Kelly loves being part of a team. She feels that has always been a team player, but she did not learn about teamwork in gym or through sports. She learned to be a team player at work. For her, work is related to collaborative activities and fitness is something that is individual.

> In my work life I am a team player. I love collaborative effort and feel like two heads are better than one. In fitness, I own it. It's mine. Team sports require concentration that I don't want to give. When I am working out I want to be able to work out whatever is on my mind.

> I think my attitudes about fitnesswere shaped by my upbringing and by my mother more than gym. My mother grew up on a lake. She was a swimmer. She was a lifeguard. She could sail a boat. She could a paddle a

---

[14] When students are included and encouraged to perform to their level of skill, team sports can fulfill this mission. See Shephard and Trudeau However, the experience is quite different for students who do not get to participate.

canoe. Before she married dad, she and a friend played 9 holes of golf every morning for several summers. She loved being outside and she loved doing things. She was an avid bowler. She was always very active.

Team sports offer the opportunity for socialization and can help development of social skills.[15] Kelly did not find that in team sports.

> I felt a sense of shame and felt it was unfair because I just couldn't do it. I was a failure. I didn't understand it then but all I needed was someone to help me. All I needed was someone to try to teach me and let me play.

Team sports in gym class do not always provide students with an opportunity to be active. Depending on the facilities, equipment, and resourcefulness of the gym teacher, students can end up sitting on the sidelines watching others play. Gym teachers often perceive that they select activities that are cooperative and challenging. Many gym teachers believe that competition is motivating. .[16] But even students who know how to be team players do not necessarily enjoy competition in gym.

Enjoyable physical activity can involve teamwork that is not competitive. Interactive and small group activities can be structured to be collaborative but not competitive. Focusing on the activity rather than the score of the game can help students learn about process and trying. But the opportunity to engage in an individual activity can help a student develop motor skills and a positive physical self-concept. In an individual activity the student has a chance to participate, sometimes in a non-competitive manner. These are also activities that can transition to adulthood. For students who are not skilled and thus do not feel able

---

[15] In reviewing sports and aggression, Nucci and Young-Shim discuss the potential positive and negative outcomes. Sportsmanship, motivation, and the ability to work as part of a team are among the positive outcomes. Aggressive behavior and acts of violence are negative outcomes that can flourish in settings that lack good leadership.

[16] Xiang, McBride and Solmon noted that although teachers may believe that their teaching approach is rooted in mastering a fitness or sport concept, the actual teaching blended mastery with performance goals. When students are involved in the learning process, they achieve better benefits. Students who do not perceive themselves as competitive or able to meet performance goals may not perform effectively as part of a team.

to compete, individual activities are enjoyable. Sitting on the sidelines makes gym feel like a waste of time.

Chapter 3

The Cheese Stands Alone:

The Process of Choosing Teams

for Gym Class Activities

All the girls would stand there. One team captain would pick and then the other; all the girls would go to one side or the other. The last one standing was always me.

Team activities in gym class inevitably involve dividing the students into one or more groups. It can be an easy process or more complex, depending on the goals of the activity and the number of students involved. For many classroom activities dividing the room in half or quarters by area, or having students count off into groups can get everyone sorted out very quickly. Of course that might mean that all of the skilled students end up on one team. In competitive activities then that skilled team will beat everyone. It seems that many of the issues regarding gym class are involved with the appropriateness of competition. If the goal of the activity is to encourage everyone to participate in a non-competitive, good sportsmanship-oriented manner, team selection should not be a problem. But it is.

Choosing teams for activities is perceived as important by some students. They want to be able to choose who they want to work with in gym. When students learn to trust their teammates and feel respected by their classmates, they enjoy gym class. [17] Teams that are chosen—rather than assigned—are often more

---

[17] Barney and Strand surveyed students about whether they could delineate between aspects of gym that were considered appropriate or inappropriate according to accepted physical education pedagogy. The authors suggest that based on the findings of the study, "certain perceptions regarding physical education...need to be corrected" 39.

cohesive and resistant to influence from someone new or different from the core group.[18] But what happens to students who are left out?

Almost everyone I spoke with recalled the trauma and drama of picking teams for activities in gym. For many people, picking teams was one of the worst aspects of gym class. Usually the bad memory involved the time-honored method of choosing captains to select each individual teammate. For students who did not get picked early in the process, it seemed to take a lot of time out of gym class. While this "the farmer in the dell" method may bring back warm fuzzy feelings from a game played in early grades on the playground at recess, in gym class it was painful.

For Barbara, playing "the farmer in the dell" at recess was fun because everyone was singing. It was a game that was more about the song than the process of selection of the farmer, wife, cow, pig, and so forth. When the same process was used in elementary school gym class, she found it humiliating.

> The gym teacher picked the captains. As I recall, they were the children with the most ability or with the most enthusiasm for whatever we were going to do. The captains would pick the children. Except the gym teacher would sometimes sort of intervene at moments and just say 'you can't have all the hard hitters. Some of them have to go over there.' I think they would try to make it more even which was good. But even just standing there waiting for somebody to pick you was just so horrible.

The people I interviewed who were not sports skilled assumed that the skilled students were not affected by the team selection process. Even though Adam was athletically skilled, picking teams in this manner was not a positive experience. He did not usually feel alienated or persecuted, but rather that process created a negative atmosphere. It very clearly created and reinforced the hierarchy in gym class.

> There was always a pecking order so the best athletes got picked first and then those who were left standing in line would be the worst athletes.

---

[18] Choi and Levine studied the impact of team dynamics on decisions. Assignment and selection of teams or strategies can influence the outcome of a team-oriented project.

Often there would be a groan if you got somebody on your team that everybody thought was a klutz or whatever.

For many people the act of choosing teams was agonizing. Simply recalling the activity made them feel uncomfortable. Eileen was a good athlete and a talented dancer. When it came time to choose teams for activities, she was often one of the captains who got to pick. "I hated it. It was awful" because she knew that someone would always end up feeling bad. As the team captain she felt that there was no way to avoid having someone end up feeling bad because they were chosen last or near the end. The athletic girls at Kelly's middle school were almost always put in charge of picking teams for gym class activities. It was the same process every time the class divided into teams.

> I was the new kid in school and not an athlete. I wasn't like them and they knew it and they made fun of me. When it came time for teams, pretty much the captain of the team and her first mate would get up there and start picking people. They would talk and whisper about you. I was always the last one picked because I was the new kid. It was an awful feeling. I was very sensitive. It was very demoralizing.

Kendra had a similar experience. Because she lacked sports skill, she was chose last. Even though all students ended up on a team, she felt the drama was unforgiving.

> Everyone eventually got picked. But I was always the last picked. It was me and somebody else. So one team would have to get the one klutz—which was me—and the other team would have to get the other klutz. Both teams were very unhappy and let you know it.

Choosing teams can be a good learning experience. Students can learn how to evaluate potential teammates for their ability to contribute to the activity. They can also learn about respect, recognition, and empathy. Because Eileen got to choose, she benefitted from the experience as a team captain. Others were not so lucky. The selection process reinforced the thought that they did not belong in gym class. As a non-skilled student George was subject to humiliation in team selection, but sometimes he had help. For him, it was not the gym teacher

attempting to create a comfortable environment in gym class. Rather it was George's cousin, the star athlete, who had compassion.

> The saving grace for me was my cousin. I had a cousin who was a very nice guy and very athletic. He was the star athlete. When they would pick captains he was always one of the captains. When he was picking teams he'd pick me a little bit earlier than last. This was very, very nice. You know I can't tell you how nice. If he wasn't captain I'd get picked very last which is so humiliating.

George's cousin came to his rescue. Perhaps out of a sense of loyalty, or maybe he had developed empathy and a sense of fairness. Some non-skilled students developed resilience from this process. Franco usually got picked last in gym class, but he did not let it bother him.

> I was not athletically inclined. Sometimes people would pick me first just for fun. That made me feel kind of cool.

Sensitive students and those who are not desirable teammates because of their lack of skill can be emotionally hurt in this process. Students like Franco and Jackie develop resilience. Jackie never got to pick a team in gym class. Like Franco, she decided that she would not let it bother her. She was able to depersonalize the experience and also understand that her lack of sports skill did not affect her ability to contribute in other areas of school. In her high school civics class they used the "farmer in the dell" method of picking teams for an activity.

> We had this one thing that I think happened mostly in like a civics class or a history class. It wasn't exactly debate team but it was similar to that. If I wasn't the captain of the team, I was one of the first ones chosen for it. My classmates perceived that I was going to be valuable to the team. It was directly opposite of what happened in gym.

Choosing leaders in gym class or team captains is considered to be appropriate by physical education experts. The idea that leaders are necessary in gym class makes it different than other classroom subjects. Other classroom subjects sometimes require students to take on leadership roles in collaborative

learning activities. Reliance on team sports in gym means that someone must assume leadership of a team to help it function properly. The issue most people recalled was not with the actual teams, rather with a team member selection process that often was perceived as having as much drama as the annual player draft of the National Football League.

Testing students on skills, ranking them, and then dividing them into teams based on the ranking is another recommended classroom management technique.[19] Theoretically the "leaders" could encourage less skilled or unenthusiastic students. Basically both approaches end up creating an exclusionary atmosphere.

What about randomly assigning teams? For some reason, that is not recommended by the experts; possibly because it may not necessarily balance out skill levels for competitive activities. This circles around to the question of the emphasis on competition in gym.

If everyone is expected to participate and be active, why highlight the skilled students? Maybe the experts who recommend this approach enjoyed being singled out in gym. Or maybe they don't want gym class to be fun. If gym is fun it might seem unimportant. Choosing teams can help some students enjoy gym. However, the risk of alienating and marginalizing students is high. Certainly the students who are picked last feel excluded even when everybody ends up on a team. The anxiety that students feel when they are waiting to be picked is very real to them. The experience is perceived as painful. For most people it does not promote an atmosphere of inclusion.

A student who does not feel that he/she belongs to a team will not reap from the expected social benefits of teamwork in gym. In the playground game, the person who is designated the "cheese" usually gets to be the "farmer" in the

---

[19] Many of the selection options viewed as appropriate by Barney and Strand encourage an elitist atmosphere. Perhaps this approach assumes that students will be motivated to try hard in gym so that they can compete effectively for a leadership role in gym class. The authors also note that practices considered inappropriate in gym have been "occurring in physical education for many years.

next round. Gym was never like that for me or many of the people I interviewed. The captains and skilled students may have been really attempting to put together a good team during the selection process. But for many of us choosing teams was about waiting for our names to be called. It involved fear of the selected activity combined with trying to not appear desperate to be picked. Ultimately, as Kendra noted, everybody ends up on a team. This time-worn process takes time away from activity in gym class and reinforces the elitist mentality that is thankfully not as prevalent in other classes.

In real life, selecting team members involves assessment, careful planning, and sometimes negotiating with another team. Usually this process does not happen in front of hopeful candidates. Perhaps gym teachers who use the "farmer in the dell" method of team selection are trying to teach their students about the process of team selection. They might also be attempting to make sure that every student is assigned to a team and that the teams have an equal number of members. Whatever the motivation, it is still used in gym class and some other places where groups must separate into teams for tasks. Recalling this process gave Adam pause for thought.

> At the time I didn't think much of it. But looking back, it was a pretty horrible way to go about it because it didn't seem that it was fostering anyone's confidence in their physical abilities nor did it seem to promote the idea of physical action and activity as a positive experience.

Chapter 4

Self Perception and Self-esteem:
How Gym Class Activities Can Impact
Confidence About Movement

On occasion my gym teacher would tell me that I was clumsy and that I didn't try hard enough. So I wouldn't try anymore.

Gym means different things to different people. It always involves sports of one type or another, so gym and sports are intimately intertwined in many memories. Sports have a purpose, are competitive, and require skill. [20] Memories of gym can bring up bad feelings for people who were not skilled at sports.

The purpose of gym is to help students acquire and develop gross motor skills needed to participate in activities of daily living, lifestyle physical activity, and the selected gym activities. Much of the gym-class motor skills have traditionally been sports focused: students need to be able to throw, catch, hit, jump, run, and walk to participate in sport. What happens to the student who cannot throw, catch, or hit a ball? Who cannot jump high enough or run? Gym can hurt their self perception and erode their self-esteem.

There are many different terms that are used to describe a person's confidence in their ability to succeed at physical activity. Physical self-perception, physical confidence, perceived competence, and self efficacy, all refer to the need for a person to feel awareness of—and confidence in—their capabilities. These feelings occur regardless of actual skill level and impact the enthusiasm with which a student will approach an activity. For example, a student who is learning

---

[20] In MacDougall, Schiller and Darbyshire research on children's experiences in physical education, sports involved competition, skills, and a purpose; but not necessarily fun 375. Exercise and fitness were distinctly different concepts that did not involve play 378.

to play basketball must have confidence in their ability to run up and down a court, dribble the ball, pass the ball, and shoot. When they lack confidence in their skill it adversely affects their motivation to try to play. A supportive climate helps to improve students feelings of competence in gym.[21]

Students arrive in gym class with different backgrounds, skill levels, and interests in sports and activity. Students who are already physically active are more likely to participate in and enjoy gym class. When students lack skill, participating in gym is difficult. They may not be able to keep up with their classmates or make a contribution to the team.

Physical activity should be pleasurable so gym class should—theoretically—help students feel good. Movement is fun. It is also a form of self-expression that can be both artistic and healthy. This gives another purpose to gym: helping students understand the relationship between physical activity and health. Regular exercise and physical activity has a favorable effect on metabolism, cardiovascular health, strength, and coordination.[22] When students do not learn how to exercise, it may affect their health and daily activities when they grow up.

When the focus of gym is on sports skills in a competitive environment, students who lack skill get lost and confused. They feel left out. Jackie was physically active at home. She was a self-described tomboy. She climbed trees, as well as played basketball and softball with her brothers and cousins. They played for fun and to be together. It was not about skill. Gym class was about skill, not fun.

---

[21] See study by Trouillard, et al. on the climate created by teacher expectation effects on student motivation in physical education. It is not surprising that a supportive environment that encourages autonomy amongst students is more empowering, thus increasing physical self perception

[22] The hallmark report by the U.S. Surgeon General on physical activity and health identified for clinicians, academics, and the public that there are physical benefits to exercise and physical activity. Subsequent research has found that the majority of adults do not exercise enough to achieve these benefits.

I always got busted for traveling or not dribbling. I didn't think anybody could do this: run and dribble the ball. I didn't think it was physically possible. Although some kids did demonstrate it was, I thought they were freaks of nature. I felt really clumsy and didn't really see the point of it \

Jackie gave up. She could not master the skills and did not see the purpose of gym class. She felt gym class was pointless and disregarded it as an irrelevant part of school. At home, she worked with her brothers training horses. This required a great deal of physical skill, but it did not relate to dribbling or kicking a ball. At home she was not clumsy.

Like Jackie, Kelly was active at home. But her recollections of gym class involve feeling physically and emotionally delicate. She described herself as a "fragile flower" that was "not cut out for this." By this, Kelly meant team sports. She did not feel that she had sufficient eye-hand coordination or athletic ability necessary to participate in the team sports activities that were used in gym class. She was active at home and her initial experience with gym class was informal. At Kelly's elementary school, her class would gather in the parking lot or the church basement for gym. They would do simple calisthenics, or jumping jacks, or count off into teams and play group activities like kickball or dodgeball. She recalls that the emphasis was on moving, participating, and having fun in a non-competitive way.

> At home we were encouraged to play and be active. Mom and Dad felt that we needed to develop imagination, to learn how to entertain yourself, and to be physically active. They wanted us to get outside and we did. We would skate up and down the sidewalk. We would skip, run, and jump rope. As a family we rode bicycles and went ice-skating. They took us to swimming lessons when we were young, mostly for safety so we could go to the neighborhood pool. We had a swing set in the backyard that we played on for hours. Mom would come outside and hang with us but we were usually left to our own devices. There was really only one rule and that was to be home before the street lights came on.

In middle school, Kelly moved to a new school in a new city. Sports were important at her new school largely because they were the only extracurricular activity. Her new school did not have drama, dance, or music programs after

school; just sports. Gym class and after-school sports were closely interrelated. When she got to her new school, she was lost.

> Gym class in middle school was totally different. I felt like I had missed something somewhere along the line when I was growing up. We did not play sports, so I did not know how to play volleyball, basketball, or softball. When you are twelve years old, thrown onto the volleyball court, and suddenly someone lobs a big scary volleyball at you. What are you going to do? Duck? That's what I did. I could not bat or serve so suddenly at my new school I was the outsider. It quickly became clear that I wasn't good at sports and I wasn't going to fit in as a result. Not in sports, not in this school.

> I had no idea where the kids at my new school learned all the skills and rules. I don't know where they got it. Maybe it came from earlier training in their school Maybe it came from their older brothers and sisters. Maybe they were just doing different things than I was doing when I was growing up. But I felt like somewhere along the line I had missed something somewhere.

Kelly's lifestyle was active and enjoyable. Her initial encounters with gym were inclusive, with an emphasis on participating. For Kelly, changing schools left her with a perceived gap in physical education curriculum and a lack of physical self-confidence. The competitive atmosphere and sports emphasis made her feel left out. She perceived that she lacked ability and had nothing to offer. It was no longer a fun experience. In Kelly's case, she got left out because she did not know how to participate.

A variety of research reports on differences in levels of physical activity in gym class for children who are inactive outside of school. The results are inconclusive and therefore somewhat confusing. For Kelly, gym class and activity at home did not relate to each other. She was unable to take what she learned in gym class and apply it outside of school. Over time, the sports-based curriculum from gym eroded her confidence to be active at home.

Darren played Little League baseball and enjoyed participating in sports at summer camp. But he felt that he was not an athlete. During our first interview, Darren bluntly stated "Early on I recognized this was not an area of proficiency."

For him, Little League baseball and summer camp were different than gym class. They were fun. The little league baseball coaches were "dads, it wasn't hyper-serious, and we didn't have uniforms." His team had players of different skill levels and the aim was to participate and have fun. Little League baseball and summer camp were not about competition, achievement, or winning. His recollection of gym was traumatic. Darren's early gym memories involve "being hit by a red, rubber ball in dodgeball, climbing a rope, and running around the baseball diamond until you puked." Darren did not find gym to be enjoyable or inspiring.

The gym class environment creates the possibility for a variety of interpretations depending on a student's skills and general level of physical activity. Younger students tend to enjoy the activities and interaction. The students may not understand the purpose of physical activity, but they enjoy movement. They perceive the emphasis to be on classroom management (playing by the rules and waiting for your turn) rather than achievement of an outcome (like hitting the ball or winning a game). Everyone participates, because participation is the goal. Perhaps because young children are developing their gross motor skills, they are at a similar ability level. In other words, gym is a more level playing field when everybody is just starting out. However, this tends to change over time. As students develop sports-based skills, a division of sorts occurs that separates skilled and unskilled students. When students are able and willing, they try harder. The students who are unskilled can feel left out.

In elementary school, Barbara was relatively typical. She enjoyed gym class, even when she did not understand the purpose of the activities.

> I loved the medicine ball. They would roll out this ball that was covered in leather and it was as big as I was. Well it was bigger in the beginning but then I grew to be bigger than it over the years. But the first time they ever rolled that out it was in kindergarten or 1st grade. It was like the size of a car to me! We would have to stand in the corner of the gym and roll it back and forth. I don't remember them telling us the point of the activity. I guess it was a strength and resistance thing involving coordination, stop

the ball, roll the ball, and work together. So the ball would come out and crush a few small children. We would laugh and scream and run around and it was really fun.

By middle school, the activities were skill-based. Barbara wanted to try but does not remember being taught how to throw, hit, or catch a ball. At that age, the students in Barbara's class were expected to know how to play the sports in gym class. Barbara did not have the skills and did not know how to participate.

I felt like I was unwanted and just totally dorky; that I never should be on a team, ever. Nothing the teachers ever did contradicted that. I wish I had learned how to participate in a group sport without it being quite so daunting. I wish they could've taught us these exercises or these activities in such a way that they weren't so daunting. Then I could have learned to enjoy it.

When students feel bad about their skills and ability to contribute to a team activity, they are not motivated to participate. They lack self-confidence and do not develop a positive physical self concept. They lack determination.[23] Kelly did not understand how to run, or why a girl should run.

They wanted us to run in the spring of 8th grade and I thought 'you've got to be kidding me.' There's no way. I don't run. I can't run. It's out of the question. No particular reason. It was just not even anywhere on the radar screen for me. I don't know why. But it just wasn't there. It was a preconceived notion I had and no one ever told me running was possible.

Kelly did not see the point in trying something that she did not understand. Running was hard for her and she did not feel it was possible. Likewise, George is not athletic. He tried to participate in sports and his gym class usually emphasized inclusion of all students. But gym did not help him develop self-confidence.

Wrestling was torture for me because I was so bad. I was so weak that they would have me wrestle against people that were in the weight class below me right. It was no challenge for them because it was like 'okay he's pinned'. It was pathetic. I didn't mind doing it. I mean it was

[23] Boiche, et al. identified three distinct motivational groups in gym. The majority of the sample was identified as possessing high or moderate levels of self-determination. Approximately 25% of the sample comprised the non-self determined group. This group was less intrinsically motivated and scored lower on performance based events.

perfectly okay. It just was so embarrassing because I was so bad. I just couldn't do it. I think it was a combination of not being aggressive, not being strong, not want to hurt someone, and not wanting to get hurt myself. So it was easier to just go along with it and get pinned and get it over with.

How do students develop physical self-confidence? By learning in a positive environment, getting an opportunity to participate, being encouraged, and feeling a sense of accomplishment. For many people, that means individual activities that emphasize fun and participation rather than competition. Expressive movement can help develop confidence. Like many people, Kelly found out that she enjoyed dance.

> I can remember being delighted my sophomore year when for one full quarter of gym we did dance. It was a lot like line dancing. But it was for coordination and movement and I was good at it and I discovered that early on and I loved it.

> I auditioned for the school musical and was cast in the chorus. We danced. It wasn't a terribly athletic pursuit but you did have choreography and you did have staging. Suddenly I felt like I belonged. Suddenly somehow that took the edge off gym class.

Kelly went on to dance in chorus and school musicals. It was creative, collaborative and involved camaraderie. Dance did not seem related to gym class. Jackie enjoyed square dancing because none of her classmates knew what they were doing. She felt like she had some company.

> One time we did this real fun thing. We practiced some kind of dance thing—like square dancing—so the boys and the girls were together. It was fun to see the boys. I envied that the boys were generally a lot more adept in gym class. We were all a bunch of klutzes.

For Jackie, everyone came down to her level. Her gym teacher had called her clumsy, and during dance she was able to see her classmates struggle at an activity for which they lacked skill. It was memorable for someone who saw herself as an outcast in gym. Barbara had a sense of accomplishment when she was able to excel at dance in gym class.

> We did some really cool Polynesian dance with bamboo poles. It's kind of hard to explain. It's like where two people would take the poles, then they would slide them together and out. You would have to jump in between them and jump out. That was a blast. It took some coordination but weirdly enough, I was the only one who could do it really well.

Dance helped Barbara's self-confidence. She did not have sports skills, but she was good at a non-sports activity. She learned that she loved to dance. At Darren's school, they had social dance in gym class. He remembers that it was a distinct departure from the usual sports activities. Like Kelly, Darren learned to dance and to enjoy dancing in chorus. That is where he learned to tap dance.

> The choreographer of our musicals was a local dance instructor in town. She was a kook. She was a former Rockette. That was her claim to fame. She would involve the whole chorus in the choreography. She would also identify a few of the kids who looked like they might be able to dance and would give us feature parts. Then we got some lessons in her dance studio. This was fun for me. I was less interested in sports by then because I was not as capable.

Dance was not a path to physical fitness for Darren, but it helped him learn to enjoy movement as self expression. Miriam did not dance in gym class. She took dance lessons after school. They never danced in her gym classes. Her mother enrolled her in dance lessons so that she would not be shy. It was different from farm work.

> There are very few things that are more fun to do then dance. I loved to tap dance. I tap danced from the time I was a little kid. Dancing kept my body alive. It kept my muscles stretched. I was very limber. As an adult I kept dancing, not for health reasons, just because it was fun to do. It always made me feel good.

Dance also made Kendra feel good, but she did not learn to dance in gym. For her gym class was about surviving until the class was over.

> By high school I had given up the notion that I would be any good at anything. I think it was over. By that point I probably wasn't utilizing the tools that the teacher in 3rd grade—or whatever—had given me. I wasn't any good and I didn't like being bad at something and being blamed for it. It's one thing if I was deliberately missing shots in gym. But I wasn't. I

was just bad and they just were like 'oh you suck.' So why would I want to be there?

Eventually, almost everyone that I interviewed discovered that exercise and physical activity can be fun. But none of them learned that in sports activities in gym class. Few have played any sports since gym class. Instead they have walked, cycled, lifted weights, swam, run, or hiked. Many have taken fitness classes like boxing, Pilates, yoga, or aerobics. The goal was to do something. It helped do what gym class did not: promote their self-esteem and physical self-confidence.

As adults, the choice of the activity and the environment where it takes place makes a big difference. While gym class was a place where making a basket, catching the ball, and scoring points mattered, individual activities like dance and gymnastics gave meaning to movement and self-expression. According to Kelly, learning to move in a meaningful way through dance "somehow made all the difference."

Chapter 5

Teachers and Teaching:

Giving Gym Teachers Adequate Training and Resources to Provide Instruction in Gym

They were coaches more than they were gym teachers. They were teaching gym because that's what they were doing when they weren't coaching a sport.

In gym class, the teacher is the gatekeeper. He or she is the organizer, coach, instructor, referee, first-aid responder, and evaluator. The opportunity for the students to be active depends—in large part—on the teacher. The prospects for a student to learn how to enjoy physical activity are also somewhat dependent on the teacher; this is because the teacher sets up the classroom. Enjoyment is important in gym. If a student does not enjoy physical activity or exercise, then the student will likely not engage in regular activity. That makes gym class different from subjects like mathematics or art.

Study of mathematics teaches problem solving along with skills like adding, subtracting, multiplying, dividing. Art teaches creativity along with appreciation for form, shape, color, and texture. Without mathematics skills, people would have difficulty managing money, monitoring time, or measuring distance. Without art skills they would have difficulty doing things like putting together a wardrobe or decorating their home. Knowledge from mathematics and art are used on a daily basis; they sort of creep into life on a subtle level.

Being physically active is different because it requires conscious effort and a sense of purpose. So, while a person might not like mathematics or art, or they have trouble balancing a checkbook or matching clothes, they still have to

handle money and get dressed in the morning. People do not necessarily have to exercise. Exercise is a personal choice.

The popular media often presents the image of gym teachers as super-fit, unintelligent, and mean or demeaning to students.[24] While this reinforces stereotypes, the consistency of these presentations does make one wonder about how gym teachers are perceived differently than teachers of other subjects. Darren and Adam both had gym teachers who bullied students in class. Erin, Miriam, Kelly, Kendra, and other subjects had gym teachers who were neither involved nor trained in physical education. The teachers appeared to lack intelligence about the subject matter and seemed unable to perform effectively in gym class.

From a professional perspective, gym teachers should provide instruction, create a positive environment, and assess what the students have learned.[25] On the surface, this is really no different than what is expected of teachers of any other subjects. But gym teachers have an unusual characteristic. They are positioned to have an extraordinary influence on the future of their students,[26] possibly more than any other teacher. People need to be taught how to exercise and encouraged to be motivated to exercise. Regular exercise is important to maintain health. The person best positioned to facilitate this is a gym teacher. If the teacher believes that gym is important, then that will be communicated to the students—overtly or covertly. However, if the teacher does not believe in the value of gym, the students will pick up on that. Unfortunately, not all teachers who are assigned to teach gym want to do it, or even believe in the importance of gym. But exercise is

---

[24] McCullick, et al. analyzed presentations of gym teachers in film over a ten-year period. they identified four basic themes: coaches and gym teachers are interchangeable, gym teachers are incompetent, teachers are bullies who humiliate students, and male teachers are portrayed as emasculated while female teachers are portrayed as butch. The authors note that gym teachers are generally not presented as pleasant, supportive characters.

[25] The evolution of educational standards has given rise to board certifications and gym class curricula. Phillips found students of board certified teachers scored higher on fitness knowledge, testing, motor skill competency and physical activity participation outside of class. This suggests that gym teachers who are trained and prepared for the gym classroom are better prepared to instruct students.

[26] Cowley's post World War II "challenge to physical education" stated that physical education teachers had both a responsibility and an opportunity to educate students for their health and well-being as well as encouraging pursuit of sports to fill the anticipated abundant leisure time 176.

important and a gym teacher's real charge is to inspire and motivate students to exercise regularly and correctly.

In some schools, teachers are responsible for teaching multiple subjects. Some classroom teachers are responsible to teach specialty courses like gym, music, and art along with the academic subjects. [27] In these situations the teachers may not be adequately prepared to teach gym. At Miriam's high school, the gym teacher taught music and gym.

> The girls' gym teacher was also the choral director. She was bad at both. She couldn't play the piano very well and we didn't learn to read music. She put in her time in the gym. We had no respect for our gym teacher as a gym teacher. Nor did we have any respect for her as a choral director.

Miriam's gym teacher did not communicate any value or importance of gym class. That might be due to inadequate training in physical education. Miriam's teacher might have been a "physically illiterate" individual.[28] Unfortunately in her case, she was passing along her lack of motor skill to her students.

For Kelly, the preparedness and the approach of her gym teachers made a big difference in her perception of class. She had three distinctly different experiences in elementary middle, and high school. Kelly's elementary school gym teacher emphasized fun and participation. Her middle school gym teacher also taught science. She did not appear to have any special training or background in physical education. So gym class was an uninspired hodgepodge of calisthenics and sports.

---

[27] In Morgan's survey of elementary school teachers on their perceptions of gym, the teachers preferred teaching all other subjects over physical education. They felt that they lacked adequate time, support, and resources to teach gym.

[28] Sawyer identifies gym teachers who lack sport and movement skills as "physically illiterate" He notes that teacher preparation programs are more " concerned about the public school child's obesity and physical fitness level than their ability to perform simple motor skills" 4 This casts the teacher in a facilitator role rather than a teacher or role model 6. His suggestion that gym teachers should be required to pass motor skill proficiency tests indicates a preference for performance-oriented gym class (which excludes non-skilled students) rather than a mastery approach (which offers inclusion opportunities for students who need to develop motor skills.)

I think she got stuck with gym and she didn't really know what to do with us. I remember her being so good at science and such a lousy gym teacher. Gym wasn't her specialty so she wasn't good at it. When I got to high school our gym teachers were athletes. They had a plan and class was structured. These women knew what they were doing.

Kelly's high school teachers were trained. They were motivated and engaged the students differently because they approached the class seriously. Kelly learned the importance of exercise. Although she still lacked sports skill and tried to get excused from gym, she understood the purpose and structure of the class.

Jackie also had a science and gym teacher in middle school. He taught her biology class. She recalls that he seemed to be a good gym teacher and a good science teacher. As a future healthcare professional, Jackie was interested in biology. She was not interested in gym. When asked if her biology/gym teacher gave her preferential treatment in gym because she was a good biology student, she replied:

I don't think Mr. B. treated me differently in gym but I approached the classes differently. I was horrible in gym but very good in biology. Science just came more naturally to me. I mean I was good in biology. Gym class was something that I had to endure for that hour of the day.

In this case, Jackie's felt that her biology/gym teacher was a good instructor. But he was unable to help her change her attitude about gym. By middle school, Jackie had already established a lack of confidence in her movement skills. Her attitudes and habits had already been formed.

In schools with dedicated physical education positions, gym teachers see students in an informal setting.[29] That setting should provide an environment to get to know the individual students. Theoretically that gives a gym teacher an excellent opportunity to get to know the students, to work with them to understand their individual goals. That should lead to helping them develop their

---

[29] Cowley proposed that the lack of formality in gym offered teachers a unique chance to engage in student-centered teaching compared to the traditional setting in the academic classroom.

own exercise and fitness plans. After all, gym class does not usually have intensive homework assignments, research papers, or written exams to grade.

Many gym teachers also coach school and community sports activities. Teachers who are sports coaches may treat gym class like a team sport. In the long term, this can create an elitist atmosphere and lead to marginalization of students who lack skills. Darren recalls his gym teachers as being prepared and knowledgeable about sports.

> I never had the impression that they were just making kids run around. In grammar school maybe; but less so in junior high and high school. But I also did not view them in the same way as I viewed my other teachers. In some ways I think their job is interesting, because it is coaching. Because they were coaches they knew some of us students much better than others. So there was some element of favoritism that would usually end up in gym.

Encouraging, and motivating students are important tools for a gym teacher if they are to succeed in getting students to be active. The teacher is a coach, but sometimes the coach must learn to be a teacher. But as Darren notes, coaches who know that some students are skilled may marginalize students who lack skill. Most of Adam's gym teachers were also coaches. Adam noticed considerable differences in his soccer coach's expertise and ability to teach gym class.

> The two that I remember the best were the head soccer coach and the head football coach. And as far as I know all they taught was gym. The quality of the instruction I received playing on the soccer team from the soccer coach was high quality. But when he was teaching gym, he knew some things but he certainly wasn't an expert in something like gymnastics. So I learned a little bit, but I wasn't receiving high quality training.

Gym teachers who have skill in one sport may not have the to teach other sports or activities. Erin's gym teacher did not have any expertise in gymnastics or tumbling, but that was an activity in her gym class. Erin did not know how to tumble, but she was expected to participate along with everyone else.

> The teacher would say 'today we're going to tumble. Line up and you do a roll-over and you do it right after that person.' I don't ever remember her demonstrating tumbling herself. The people that taught us the most were the cheerleaders because they used some rudimentary tumbling back then in cheerleading.

The students in Erin's class were drawn into an instructional role because of their own expertise. It was unclear to Erin why tumbling was part of gym class if her teacher did not have adequate experience. Perhaps it was because her school had the basic equipment needed for tumbling. At Kendra's high school, the football coach was one of her gym teachers.

> They basically turned gym class into a study hall while they watched video tapes of the football team all the time. They didn't teach us anything. I should also say that our football team was so bad that they lost the last year I was in high school to a team that hadn't won a game in thirty years.

In Kendra's case, the football coach may have had adequate training and equipment to teach gym class, but for some reason chose not to teach. A bad gym teacher can have an effect on the student's health for the rest of his or her life. How do students identify "good" and "bad" teachers? A good teacher clearly articulates the expectations of the class and treats students equitably. A bad teacher may not communicate his or her expectations, or facilitate participation by all students, or treat all students equally regardless of skill level.

What the teacher expects sets the stage for the gym classroom. When students perceive an expectation that they should be skilled—and they lack skill—they are unable to participate appropriately. If a student perceives that they are expected to participate—to the best of their ability—they are more likely to be motivated to try.

Jackie was not motivated to try in gym. She felt that her gym teachers did not expect much from her because she was not skilled at sports. Kendra admits that "my coordination did not kick in until college." It was difficult for her to perform sports-skills that were necessary to participate in gym. When gym class

performance is based on sports participation—rather than general physical activity—unskilled students get lost. Not only do they lack ability, they may lack an understanding that exercise and physical activity do not necessarily mean sports participation.

The teacher's beliefs and attitudes influence classroom management as well as the ability of the students to learn. Since she did not have gym in elementary school, Erin looked forward to high school gym class. She thought that gym was going to be important. Unfortunately the classroom environment was not conducive to learning about exercise and physical activity.

> I found out fairly quickly that the gym teacher played favorites with people. I was not a favorite. The teacher picked the tallest girls—a pair of twins—who spent a lot of time playing volleyball or 5 on 5 basketball.

> Sometimes--I remember when it was cold outside--the teacher would have us sit in the bleachers doing homework. That's when I learned to play poker, because I could get my homework done really quickly. The teacher would not supervise us so we would gamble away our lunch money.

Erin and her classmates were resourceful. They used gym class time and their own resources to learn a different skill. Regardless of whether Erin was watching other girls play basketball or she was involved in a poker game, Erin was not physically active in gym class.

Kendra's earliest memory of gym class was positive. She got help with sports skills after school. The experience involved a substitute teacher.

> In second or third grade I had been evidently not very good at softball or something so she took me and another girl out after school and put the softball on a stand. She helped us learn to hit the ball from the stand. And then she tossed the ball to us and helped us hit it when it was coming at us. Unfortunately, that teacher was a substitute. She did not stay around very long.

Kendra appreciated the attention, she learned from the experience. She also learned that a substitute was much more interested than her regular gym teacher.

General feedback from gym teachers is perceived to be good.[30] Singling out talented students as examples is often used in gym class, but it can make students feel bad about themselves if their names are never called. Students who lack skill are thought to get more attention from teachers, but it is not always beneficial attention.

Tracy and George both suffered from allergies that affected their cardiorespiratory fitness and therefore their ability to run. Tracy remembers her high school gym teacher yelling at her to try to run faster while she labored to circle the outdoor track. George's middle school gym teacher told him that he could stop running during a fitness test even though all of the others students were finished. Both Tracy and George were embarrassed to be singled out because it called attention to their allergies. Tracy really wanted to try to keep up, but the gym teacher did not teach her anything about how to train and condition to develop cardiorespiratory fitness. She was left behind.

Gym teachers are expected to be prepared, cooperative, dependable, as well as respectful and sensitive.[31] Respect and sensitivity are important for students who do not like to exercise or are not skilled at sports. Respect and sensitivity from a teacher can help create a tolerable—perhaps enriching— environment in gym class. In other words, mathematics and art teachers do not marginalize students the way some gym teachers do.

The gym teacher as an elitist was a common theme among the people I interviewed. However, the elitist attitude was not characteristic of most of the other teachers that they were able to recall. Other classrooms were remembered as inclusive, even when the feedback was negative.

---

[30] Barney and Strand surveyed students on their perceptions of appropriate teaching and assessment methods in gym class. While students believed that it was alright for teachers to given general comments and feedback to the class, the authors report that is not a recommended practice for gym teachers.

[31] Lund, et al. surveyed gym teacher education faculty on important characteristics for gym teachers. They identified ten characteristics/dispositions as essential, but noted that many teacher education programs did not evaluate potential gym teachers based on these characteristics.

In cases where gym teachers were adequately educated and had access to facilities and equipment, the students still often felt a lack of instruction. Marty's school had a gym with a basketball court. He desperately wanted to learn how to play basketball. When it came time to play:

> It was more or less 'here's a ball now shoot' rather than showing us how to do things. I sat on the bench during practice time. So I never really learned. I enjoyed playing basketball but I never really had the instruction on how to do it.

Unlike many students in gym, Marty was motivated and willing to try. But, he was marginalized by his teacher. For students like Marty, Erin, Kelly, Miriam, Kendra, and I the gym teacher was not a coach, instructor, or facilitator. The teacher became a barrier because of their lack of training, elitist attitude, or shortage of offering positive feedback. Perhaps our gym teachers were kind, well-meaning individuals but some of us were let down.

It may seem unfair that movies portray gym teachers as drill sergeants or incompetent fools.[32] But gym teachers are given the opportunity to teach and are responsible for their classrooms. Is art really imitating life; or does life imitate art? In other words, are the media caricatures of gym teachers accurate, or do gym teachers act out because that is what society allows? The portrayal of gym teachers in an unfavorable light may seem undeserved, but does seem to reflect the experiences of some students.

The purpose of examining recollections of gym class is not to bash physical education teachers. But rather to consider the potential impact of physical education on students who did not succeed. For those students, sometimes the teacher was unable or unwilling to provide instruction to help the student meet fitness goals. Forcing students to sit on the sidelines to watch team activities was the norm in many recollections. This was the only class many people can recall where this was viewed as an accepted method of instruction.

---

[32] See McCullick, et al.'s analysis of the portrayal of gym teachers in films.

Considering the potential presented by gym class and the role of the gym teacher, Kendra noted:

> Throughout school the gym teachers could have made a difference, but they didn't for the most part.

Chapter 6

Marginalization and Avoidance:
How Students Get Sidelined in Gym

We would play poker while the other girls played basketball and the gym teacher did not care.

When asked about gym class, the first thing Cathy said was "marginalization." As an educator and clinical psychologist, Cathy noted that the teaching strategies her gym instructors used in class created a two-tiered system. Students were divided into groups based on skills; non-skilled students were often excluded from participating in sports activities. Since Cathy was not a skilled athlete, she was sent to sit on the sidelines. For her, that was her most enduring memory of gym class.

Kelly also spent a lot of time on the sidelines in middle school. Kelly was not skilled at sports, did not know the rules of the game, and was usually picked last when teams were chosen. The team captains would select the girls who got to play. Her gym teacher did not insist that the teams make substitutions, so the girls who did not get to play sat and watched.

Looking back I remember that there were a fair number of us who sat on the sidelines. I wasn't the only one. I just felt like it at the time. Eventually I think we bonded. But there was a pecking order and we were not part of it.

Cathy and Kelly's experiences were not at all unusual. Erin had a similar experience at her small town high school.

The teacher picked her favorites—who were also the tallest—and they spent a lot of time playing basketball. About twenty girls would sit courtside while the other ten girls played. We would hang out in the bleachers, study, and do homework.

I could get my homework done quickly so that's when I learned to play poker. We gambled away our lunch money which was about $2.50 for the entire week.

For Cathy, Kelly, and Erin, the class was about spending the required amount of time in gym. It was not about exercising or learning about the health benefits of physical activity. It was not about collaboration and participating. Instead, gym class was about waiting and watching other students play. It was about being marginalized and excluded.

Exclusion is a known problem in gym class, but it is not generally identified as a problem in other academic areas. When exclusion or marginalization is addressed, it is usually flipped and discussed as the need for inclusion of all students.[33] Whatever "spin" is put on the topic, marginalization is a problem in gym.

Preferential treatment for skilled students not only makes non-athletic students feel bad, it interferes with their ability to learn in gym. Basically if a student does not get to do an activity, he/she will not be able to achieve the goals of gym class (i.e. improving motor skills, learning to take turns, or developing a personal fitness plan.)

When schools have limited resources in terms of equipment and facilities it is difficult to involve all students in a single activity. There are ways to address this, but gym teachers need to be creative. One option is to choose non-competitive activities like aerobics, boot-camp, or social dance that can involve all students. Another option is to play sports like flag football or softball that can accommodate large numbers of players on each team. Still another possibility is to forego one large regulation game in favor of scaled down games using multiple teams. At Darren's middle school, when they played basketball in gym class the

---

[33] Hardin comes close when he notes that racial and ethnic prejudice is not acceptable. Adaptive physical education prepares teachers to instruct students with physical disabilities. While disability is distinctly different from lack of skill, students with disabilities are required to be included in gym. Students who lack skill are not.

game was modified to include everyone. They had several half-court games playing simultaneously. Darren got to play basketball

For non-skilled students, motivation is important to get them to be active. Sending students to the sidelines makes gym class seem like competitive sports. Perhaps this happens because many gym teachers are also coaches. Maybe they confuse the purpose of gym with the goal of sports: winning.[34] Sending unskilled students to the sidelines does not inspire them to become more skilled and aspire to get into the game. For those of us who sat on the sidelines in gym class, it was anything but inspirational or motivating.

While I loved to play basketball at home, I was not a very good player. In middle school gym class, basketball was about doing things right and playing the game well. I remember the teacher and my teammates getting exasperated with me when I could not remember who I was supposed to guard or could not sink a shot. When I did not succeed at making a positive contribution to the game (which was most of the time) I was sent to the sidelines. Playing basketball with my friends in the neighborhood was about having fun and encouraging each other. Basketball in gym class was about the athletic girls. What I learned from gym class was that sports were for other people, not me.

Students who perceive that they are competent in sports or activities will try to participate and succeed in that activity. Those who lack self-confidence are less likely to be motivated. It is pretty logical that a student will not try if they think they will be unable to succeed. Jackie remembers sitting on the sidelines watching other girls play basketball in gym class. She decided that the best way to cope with gym class was by giving up. She did not want to feel hurt so she just did not try to play well.

Unless they needed a lot of fouls, I wasn't put in the game very often. If the teacher encouraged me it probably didn't last very long because I

---

[34] Treanor and Hauser note that when gym teachers are dually hired as coaches, their evaluation and reappointment to their job is often based on whether they can produce a winning team rather than their performance as a gym teacher. In that situation, they are likely to put more effort into coaching rather than teaching gym.

probably wasn't very enthusiastic about it. I can't say that it was the teacher's fault for not encouraging me because I didn't leap at the opportunity. She probably just thought well I didn't really care so she picked somebody who did care.

Inclusiveness in gym class is problematic, but interestingly enough it is usually not a problem in other academic areas. So why is marginalization a problem in gym? Looking back, Kendra feels that her gym teachers had a different approach and attitude than teachers of other subjects.

They were probably well-meaning folks who did great in gym. Maybe they always had a good time so they don't see people were being marginalized in activities where they were "good" and "bad."

The concept of achievement is important in education, but especially vital in gym class. For a student to have a sense of achievement in gym class, he or she must successfully meet the gym teacher's expectations. Basically, the gym teacher must outline the goals of gym class. These goals are rooted in the curriculum and manifested in the environment of the class that is set by the teacher.

For Lizzie, sports and exercise at summer camp were different than gym class. "They didn't yell at us at camp, but they did in gym." Gym class focused on the performance-oriented goals at Lizzie's school rather than participating. A gym class can either focus on performance or the idea of mastery. Lizzie's performance-oriented gym class emphasized competition and superiority; whereas her summer camp took a mastery-oriented approach that encouraged individual development. Gym classes that involve exclusion of non-skilled students are performance-oriented. That sets the stage for marginalization. Thus a gym class that aimed to prepare students for lifetime physical activity would need to be mastery-oriented; even if sports are the primary means of activity.

Students may avoid participating in gym because they fear getting yelled at or they lack confidence. Sometimes students do not understand what to do or

how to do it.[35] A determining factor in student motivation to participate is expectations set by the teacher and the gym class environment. They might be afraid of getting hurt or being embarrassed. Marty thought high school gym class looked rough and dangerous. It did not look fun so he did not want to take part.

> I found the gym teacher before the semester. I asked if he had chosen a towel boy. The gym teacher said "what's a towel boy?" I said I get all the towels out for the students, distribute them, collect them, fold them, and put them away. Somehow I managed to sell the gym teacher on that idea. So I listened to a radio program while I folded towels. There had never been a towel boy in gym before that and I don't think there ever was after. I never participated in any gym activities, and I got an A.

Simone tried to avoid gym class altogether. She hated gym. She recalls begging her mother for notes. "I was always having my period." Kelly also tried to avoid gym by using her menstrual cycle as an excuse. Both Simone and Kelly essentially banished themselves to the sidelines. For them it was a more familiar place than trying to fit into a role on a sports team. Barbara worked hard to stay out of the way in gym.

> I remember praying to sit on the sidelines. I was always just frightened out of my mind any time I had to sit there and wait to play; it was like a death sentence. During softball or kickball I stood in the outfield. I inhabited the quarter way, way, way behind first base. As far away from anywhere a ball might go. I just went as far away as possible.

Like Barbara, Kendra liked softball because it offered the opportunity to stay away from the game. She could act like she was participating, but not be involved at all.

> I was delighted to be put way out in the outfield because I could sing. If it was a nice day, I would stand out there and sing to myself. I was happy to be as far away as possible.

---

[35] Silverman, Kulinna, and Crull studied the impact of tasks/skills, presentation and teacher accountability on student's ability to perform skill tests. Giving students explicit instructions and the opportunity for multiple trials or attempts at a task/skill helps students to understand the concept and perform the task/skill. When students know they are being graded on the ability to execute a task/skill, they display better performance.

Why did Barbara and Kendra want to be away from activity? They feared failure and humiliation. Darren did not fear failure or humiliation, but he knew he did not belong in the infield.

> Whenever we played baseball I was an outfielder. I didn't play bases. Playing the bases was something that more athletically-inclined students did. Anybody who wasn't athletically inclined was sent out into the outfield.

While Darren did not mention feeling excluded, his role was clear to him. Stay out of the way of the game. Even though they were in the game, Barbara, Kendra, and Darren were excluded. Adam was lucky that he was a good athlete, but his gym class did have activities that marginalized non-skilled students. He understood why a non-skilled student might want to avoid participating in gym.

> Gym was not a bad experience for me because I was among the luckier ones, I mean lucky because I don't think of it as some great achievement or anything. I was fortunate enough to be fairly capable at most of what they asked me to do. I remember distinctly that it bothered me that we had classes where somebody might look bad, be awkward, or get hurt. But I think humiliation was more of a worry then physical injury. Kids in my generation put a big emphasis on humiliating non-athletes.

Samuel was also one of the lucky ones. He was not athletic, but he did not have any problem in gym class. It was not inspiring, nor was it problematic. He showed up for class, participated in activities, and went on to his next class. Although Samuel did not learn much from gym he was not excluded or humiliated in gym class. Since gym class was "not really an issue." he did not try to avoid gym.

Marginalizing students can lead to feelings of humiliation and humiliating non-skilled students can make them feel marginalized. Samuel had a positive environment, but many students did not. Barbara's teacher laughed along with her classmates when she failed to hit a softball in elementary school. Kendra's teacher did not respond to her request for help dealing with bullies and gave her a low grade. Some students feel humiliation when excluded from participation in an

activity. Marty desperately wanted to be a good basketball player, but he rarely got to play in gym class because the teacher selected who got to play. Erin also aspired to be a good basketball player because her mother played on a championship basketball team in school. Since Erin was not usually selected by the gym teacher to play, she felt excluded, disappointed, and humiliated.

Gym teachers should be sensitive to the abilities of students. When some students cannot be included in activities, it should not always be the same students who are excluded. Marginalization and avoidance are intimately interconnected. Students who are excluded from activities do not learn how to participate. They do not develop the skills or knowledge that enables them to participate effectively. That can lead them to avoid activity. Basically if they do not know what to do, or they cannot do it right, there is little point in trying. George was happy sitting on the sidelines when other people played football.

> I didn't mind sitting on the sidelines during football. I was so afraid of getting tackled. As long as I didn't have to play I was fine. I never felt really adept at whatever we were doing in gym.

Chapter 7

Staring Down the Bullies:

Teasing and Acting Out In and Around the Gym

The sports clique started picking on me in gym class because of my lack of athletic ability. From there it escalated to other parts of school.

Bullies are everywhere: demeaning, teasing, doing physical harm, and ostracizing.[36] It is estimated that up to half of school-aged children are involved somehow in bullying incidents in school. Research has different classifications for bullies. Essentially it can be viewed as a spectrum ranging from *bullies* to *victims*, with *bully-victims* in between. A fourth group is considered *not involved* because they do not identify as a participant or victim. [37]

Barbara recalls:

There were some children who just made fun of everybody. They were the bullies. Some of them definitely were the ones that always had to have all the attention. They were not taught that everybody should participate and everybody might have a level of skill and that's okay. They were probably taught that either you're at the head of the line or you're shit. They were at head of the line.

Barbara could be classified as not involved in bullying. Somehow, Barbara managed to avoid the bullies at her school. She was able to identify them and stay out of their way. That might be because she lacked some of the traits that are commonly found in bullying victims.

Generally victims of bullying are perceived as being different in some way from their classmates. Victims of physical bullying are often smaller in stature or

---

[36] Bullying exists in many different forms. Victims of bullying report higher incidences of psychosomatic illnesses. See Gini and Pozzoli.

[37] Menesini, et al. suggest that victims of bullying and bully/victims can become stuck in a chronic role. Individuals in these two groups are more likely to suffer from anxiety and depression.

physically weaker than the bullies. Victims of verbal and emotional bullying are often shy, sensitive, or quiet.. Sometimes taunting and teasing relate to the student's lack of ability, while other times it is because a student is somehow perceived as different. Students who have difficulty learning as well as those with special academic or physical needs are often victims of bullying.

Kendra is muscular and tall. Because of her height, people frequently assume that she is a basketball player. But Kendra was not an athlete in high school or middle school. Her most vivid memory of gym class was "scarring" for her.

> In high school I was emotionally tortured over volleyball. I was tall but I was terrible. Unlike baseball or softballwhere they'd put me out in way outfield and I couldn't hear what people were saying about mein volleyball the trash talk was right up next to me. I don't think these girls knew me. To them I was an anonymous moose who couldn't do anything.

> The girls in gym were nasty to me—not because I was tall—but because I was bad. I don't think they knew height was supposed to be a helpful thing in volleyball. They were just like (gasp): 'Oh my god she's in my way. I could've hit the ball if she wasn't there. If she would move I would've hit it and we would've won the game. She lost it for us.'

> When volleyball came up I refused to play because people were mean to me. The teacher and I talked in the hallway. I told her why and she said "okay you don't have to play." I said I will do anything else by myself, whatever you want but I won't do that. She didn't assign me anything else. She didn't do a lecture on sportsmanship or talk to anybody about being nicer to me. She just gave me a D because I wouldn't play.

Kendra was not small for her age or physically weak, but she was different from the bullies. She did not understand until after high school that "height was supposed to be an advantage in volleyball." She was in advanced academic courses and played in band. She excelled in other areas of school, just not gym.

A lack of sports skill was what set Kelly apart from her classmates. She loathed gym. For her, bullying by her female classmates started in 7th grade gym class and spilled out into other areas of school.

I was from out of state. Instead of being curious or intrigued by me, they just decided to ostracize me. I couldn't play sports and I spoke differently. I wasn't like them so they made fun of me.

I remember one of them saying to me "I heard you moved here because your dad died?" I just looked at her and said "yes." She was taunting me; making fun of me because my father died. I remember thinking "you don't understand but someday you will." In high school her father passed away and I felt sorry for her. But I also thought "ouch, I didn't wish for that."

Sometimes gym creates opportunities for bullying in the design of the curriculum. For example, Adam does not fit the profile of a bully, but he had the opportunity to be a bully while playing dodgeball in gym class.

We called dodgeball "murderball." I used to love playing that game because I liked to throw, I liked to catch, and I was kind of quick. The goal was to figure out who can't get out of the way and who can't catch it. There was one girl who had a strabismus. Her glasses were really thick and her eyes were crossed a bit. If you threw the ball at her she was automatically going to get hit. It would've taken a miracle for her to catch the ball. In fact, it would've taken a miracle for her to get out of the way of the ball. There was another girl who was also extraordinarily slow of foot.

When the game would start, the boys who could throw well would quickly get the ball and they'd just wing it as hard as they could at the easiest kids to hit. Almost invariably it was one of those girls. In those days we didn't have a lot of games that accented what the girls probably were better at than the boys. Almost everything we played then involved physical power. Physical power played a big role in it. Not too many girls could throw at that age.

Adam did not recall the gym teacher doing anything to protect the girl who was unable to focus her eyes or the girl who moved slowly. He does recall playing dodgeball on many occasions in gym. Playing games like dodgeball can lead some students to act aggressively.[38] But bullies are not always the sports crowd. The bullies at Darren's school were not athletically skilled students.

---

[38] Some activities encourage singling out individual students for unfair treatment. In dodgeball the goal of the game is to eliminate players one-by-one.

They were, in fact, the kids who were completely not involved. The kids who cut class all the time; who didn't do sports; who didn't do any extracurricular activities, but, they were still forced to do gym. They were mean in gym class, the locker room, hallways, and everywhere around the school.

At his school the bullies were mean in gym class, but it was not about their superiority. Students were sometimes pushed out of the locker room into the hallway wearing little clothing. Most of Darren's high school classes were advanced placement, so he did not have academic classes with the bullies at his school. But bullying still took place in gym and extended to other areas of school.

Bullying most often occurs in areas of the school where students are unsupervised (hallways, restrooms) or are able to move about freely (cafeteria, gym). The gym locker rooms presented opportunities for bullies. Adam was often shaken down for money in gym.

There were some rough guys in the locker room and I always wanted to get out of there with my money. I put my wallet in my hall locker. I never took it to gym. I went into the locker room, changed, and ran out in a hurry. Because these guys wanted whatever money you had. They wanted anything that you put in that locker. I kept my locker locked and didn't carry much cash. I always found it advantageous to just get in and out of there in a hurry. I never remember losing any clothing, but I would never keep anything valuable down there or anything that I wanted to walk away with.

Teachers are generally alert to bullying in schools[39] but may not always be aware of the extent of the behaviors. Bullying may be emotional, verbal, or physical. Emotional bullying may involve teasing, ostracizing, or spreading rumors. Verbal bullying may include teasing as well as threats and name calling. Hitting, shoving, kicking, and stealing are examples of physical bullying. Physical bullying would be the easiest type for a teacher to identify, but it is less common than emotional or verbal bullying. At Barbara's schools:

---

[39] According to Totura, et al., student self-reports and teacher reports of suspected bullying are often in agreement.

There were no bullies in math class. There were only children who could do their homework and children who couldn't. There were no music bullies. There were no English bullies. There were no art bullies. There were no bullies except in gym and at recess. That was it. The only time you could get your butt kicked.

Once a child becomes a victim of bullying, he or she is likely to stay in that role. Both Kendra and Kelly felt helpless facing the gym class bullies. Neither recalled receiving any help from their gym teacher. What is it about gym class that intimately links it with bullying? Environment, elitism, and opportunity.

George was a very good tetherball player. Unfortunately he "got socked in the stomach by a kid that I used to play with because I beat him." This one incident does not qualify as bullying, but it does illustrate opportunities for physical harm. Since gym class involves physical activity, it is a ripe arena for physical bullying. But it did not appear to occur in gym as often as the other types. This may be due to sensitivity and good classroom management by the gym teacher.

Kendra and Kelly could be classified as *victims* of bullying, Barbara and Darren usually managed to be *not involved*. Adam would have been a *bully-victim*. While hitting helpless girls with a ball seemed somewhat harmless to Adam, he was young, and was not able to see things from the girls' point of view. Dodgeball was not about moving around and being active, it was about making less-skilled kids feel bad.

There are many differing explanations for why kids become bullies and bullies come in all shapes and sizes. However, some shared characteristic of bullies include being psychologically strong and lacking supervision at home.[40] Bullies and victims are both male and female. Traditionally bullies are

---

[40] In a study of characteristics of bullies, Jankauskiene, et al. attempted to correlate psychosocial, demographic, and socioeconomic factors with bullying behavior. Although it is known that males and females may be bullies or victims, their study noted that middle school males who were teased and reported being unhappy were more likely to be bullies themselves.

characterized as male, athletic, and popular among their peers.[41] Regardless of the bully's identity, when bullying occurs in gym class or in the locker room the gym teacher is a bystander.

Sometimes the gym teacher is the bully Gym teachers who yell at or demean students, and who use exercise and physical activity as a punishment, are engaging in bullying behaviors. Franco's high school gym teacher made the losing teams in volleyball do sit-ups and push-ups while the winning team watched. George's high school gym teacher would single him out to the whole class when he did not do something right in gym. One of my gym teachers made fun of me on the basketball court because I lacked skills and knowledge in the game.

Giving individual students specific feedback and suggestions on improving performance is considered appropriate by experts. But spotlighting an individual in front of the class is degrading, especially when the student is not skilled at the activity. One of George's gym teachers used to call him out in front of class for his lack of skill. Students who lack adequate skill really expect—and deserve—instruction so that they can succeed. Otherwise, they fall behind their peers.

Placing an emphasis on winning can encourage bullying in gym because it promotes aggressive behavior. There is a theory that vigorous activity can help to serve as an outlet for aggression.[42] It appears to be a delicate balance.

Cathy's daughter came home from school one day and asked her "why is everybody angry and yelling in gym class?" Cathy, a clinical psychologist, did not have an explanation for her daughter because she did not think a seven-year old could understand testosterone. Both men and women's bodies produce

---

[41] Victims of bullying are often identified as being somehow different. Since gym class emphasizes sports skills, the traditional picture for a gym class bully is of an individual who excels at sports. Aluede, et al. also note that peer reinforcement encourages bullies in their behavior. This group interaction may lead the bullies to believe that their actions are somehow harmless.
[42] See Nucci and Young Kim for a review of theories on aggression and sportsmanship. It is unclear whether aggressive behavior is instinctual, learned, or a combination of both.

testosterone, but different characteristics are associated with high levels.[43] Exercise is known to increase testosterone and androstenedione levels in males. Testosterone is an androgenic hormone that is responsible for sexual characteristics. Androstenedione is steroid that is a precursor for testosterone. High testosterone in males is associated with risky behavior. Use of steroid supplements will cause increased systemic levels of androstenedione and testosterone and also is linked with aggressive behavior.

Steroid supplementation is not common in gym class, but physiological alterations do occur during exercise. It is necessary for gym teachers to monitor overly aggressive behaviors like physical aggression and yelling. Although yelling can be motivating in some situations (e.g. cheering is yelling), it can also be demeaning. It depends on the words and the context. Yelling at students in a demeaning way can lead them to avoidance in gym. Like Cathy's daughter's school, yelling in gym was frequent at Lizzie's middle school. There the gym teachers yelled at the students and the students yelled at each other.

Abusive behavior and aggression are hallmarks of bullying, while good sportsmanship is part of healthy competition. Teaching students to participate and play with an emphasis on inclusion can help to create a level playing field in gym. When bullies are allowed to act out, it interferes with the ability for students like Lizzie and Kelly to function at all in gym, much less to enjoy the class.

Bullying is not considered to be an isolated incident but rather something that occurs repeatedly over a period of time. In other words, hitting a child with a ball once could be an accident or isolated malicious event. Hitting a child with a ball repeatedly, even in the context of a game, is demeaning and may cause physical or emotional harm. This circles back around to the environment created in gym class. For Darren, the selection of the activities and the lack of intervention by the gym teacher played a large part.

---

[43] The effect of exercise on hormones and their role in movement is discussed in detail in Borer's text.

In dodgeball the kids who could throw would throw hard and there were some who actually would compete with each other to see how hard they could throw the ball to hurt someone. It's just a sadistic game.

Chapter 8

Testing 1-2-3:

Grading and the Use of Fitness and

Skills Tests in Gym

I loved getting my gym grades because they always pulled up my academic grades. It was easy as cake. All I had to do was show up, get dressed, and play.

Evaluation in school attempts to capture whether information has been received, processed, and understood on some level. In the words of one of my graduate school advisors: "we have to see if there is learning going on in physical education." Basically schools are accountable to provide evidence that students are learning. For gym, this evidence is sometimes needed to rationalize the continued inclusion of gym in the curriculum

Gym class involves a process (being physically active) and a product (physical fitness).[44] Traditionally gym has operated on the assumption that students had the opportunity to exercise in class and that somehow this would motivate them to be physically active outside of class. The sum total of all of this exercise and physical activity was that the student would be physically fit. Gym class relies on integration of knowledge and participation with one underlying fundamental assumption: that all children have capability.[45] Students who lack physical self-confidence or sports skill are afraid of being poorly evaluated in

---

[44] Exercise and physical activity do not necessarily result in physical fitness. See Mood, Allen and Morrow. The process(being active) can help the student to become physically fit under the right circumstances.

[45] Silverman, Keating and Phillips state the obvious when they note that anyone can be active or play a game if they know what to do.

gym class.[46] This affects their ability to participate in gym class as well as their perception of physical activity and exercise.

There are multiple methods used in grading. Some subjects evaluate using qualitative variables—like creativity, participation, and effort; others grade on quantitative variables—like multiple choice, true/false, or matching tests. A combination of qualitative and quantitative testing is also sometimes used. For example, an essay in language class might be graded using a rubric that details expected form and content. An overall grade for music class might be based on ability to play a musical instrument (qualitative) and knowledge of the history or theory (quantitative.)

Gym classes may be graded in different ways including qualitative or quantitative. Qualitative grading might be based on the gym teacher's perception of a student's motivation, participation, enthusiasm, or improvement in a sport or activity. Quantitative grading could be based on attendance, dressing for class, knowledge of sports rules or the benefits of different aspects of physical fitness, and skill tests.

Traditionally gym class has been graded on attendance, appropriate attire, and playing by the rules. Grades in gym class are rarely based solely on the results of physical fitness tests for obvious reasons.[47] The lack of physical fitness among students is foremost among them. This is perhaps one reason why the place of gym in schools is sometimes in jeopardy.[48]

Testing and grading students should be based on the objectives of the course. The goal of gym class has changed over the years and that is sometimes—

---

[46] Fear of negative feedback from the gym teacher is intimidating for some students. This fear can interfere with their physical self-perception as well as their motivation to participate. See Ridgers, Fazey and Fairclught.

[47] See Welk and Schaben. If performance on standardized fitness tests were the sole grading rationale, then gym class would not be fair. This is especially true in a sports-based curriculum when the components of physical fitness are not reviewed and students do not have the opportunity to engage in activities that promote individual physical fitness.

[48] Essentially, if physical education is not living up to the objectives and expectations it is considered to be a soft subject and have no place in the curriculum. This is often the rationale presented for cuts to physical education funding and class time.

but not always—reflected in the grading scheme. If gym class in the primary grades centers around the acquisition of motor skill, then the grade should reflect that. Usually this is done with some type of fitness testing. Difficulties arise when students have motor difficulty or are unable to meet national or state fitness test standards. Ideally the grade should have some allowance for effort and perseverance. This would help motivate students to participate and try.

When the goal of gym class is for students to understand the benefits of exercise and participate in regular physical activity to promote health, then the gym class grade should be based on just that. For many people, the how and why of grading in gym was quite different than their other classes. According to Barbara, participating was important in gym at her school:

> We were all nagged to accomplish a minimum and to participate to a minimum level. But I think that the bar was set pretty low. I don't think it was thought of as necessarily important. It was important for us to read, write and do math. It was important to come to school. But there were certain things that they just didn't put that much energy into. Like gym.

> We were graded in gym class as we were graded in all of our subjects. The teacher did some sort of assessment, like: can you touch your toes, do the hop, skip, and jump, or climb up the rope? They would grade you based on your participation attempts or whether you were a behavioral problem using the same form that they used for everything,

> It wasn't very specific. It wasn't about meeting fitness goals or whether we lacked coordination and needed help. Nothing like that. They just sort of marked off these little boxes.

The need to do something in gym was at the forefront of Barbara's memory, but the purpose of gym class was not clear. Neither was the basis of grading. Barbara did receive an evaluation in gym, but her course grade did not reflect her abilities or participation. She always passed gym. Barbara was not a good student in mathematics which was evident in her grades for that class. For Barbara, gym class had a spot in her course plan but she was not taught that gym was a priority.

At Erin's school, gym involved knowledge content but little physical activity. The gym teacher insisted that the students learn the rules of tennis and bowling and how to score. Erin recalls being tested on sports rules, but not actually playing games. Her gym teacher seemed to lack skills and training in physical education. So it is possible that her teacher was just trying to find course content.

Darren broke his thumb playing lacrosse in high school gym so he had to sit out that term. Instead of playing, officiating, or doing anything active, he sat in the office the entire term writing a paper about lacrosse. Samantha remembers being graded on changing clothes and participating in high school gym. It was nothing compared to her academic courses. Samantha was in an advanced, college preparatory math and science tract in high school. Thankfully, her grades in gym class were as high as her other classes so gym did not "ruin" her grade point average. Adam was also graded on attendance, attire, and participating.

> Grades were a general source of competition in high school because they would post honor roll. But at my school, being a bad student wasn't as embarrassing as being a bad athlete. Luckily I got good grades in gym.

Most of my gym class experience was graded on being there. You were expected to show up for class, participate in (or watch) some sporting event, and go on with your day. Usually everyone passed no matter what they did in class. You got the same grade for sitting on the bench watching basketball or volleyball as you did if you played and won the game. What was important in high school gym was showing up and dressing appropriately. It was a rather unique grading system compared to every other course I took in school.

High school gym class grades were based on accumulated points. We received twenty points every time we showed up for gym class and dressed: ten points for the hideous powder-blue gym suit, five points for the socks, and five points for the shoes. It was about showing up and putting on the costume. Accumulate enough points and you could pass without necessarily breaking a sweat. I remember spending a lot of time sitting in the bleachers wearing my

powder-blue gym suit during my regular gym class. We were required to accumulate a certain number of points to receive a passing grade. If we were home sick from school, or forgot our gym clothes, we were not awarded those points. In that event, there were a few ways we could make up points that quarter if we were sick from class: 1) go to gym during a study period, put on the gym costume and sit in the bleachers and watch someone else's class, or 2) go the gym during a study period without wearing the gym costume and watch class for partial credit. I am not sure what we were expected to accomplish if we watched a gym class, but it was not much different than my normal activity. My last quarter in gym we were awarded points for winning events. It was the only time I recall receiving credit for actually doing anything in gym.

I usually managed to meet my gym class obligation since we were allowed a few absences from class and I was rarely absent from school. But I do remember sitting in the bleachers watching other gym classes to make up the points. Good grades were important in school. Something went wrong the quarter that I failed gym. Since it was the only term that I could recall being graded on an achievement, I could only assume that I was not worthy of that achievement. I knew that I had been on the winning badminton team, even though my contribution was probably minimal. At least I could take solace in knowing that we were not usually graded on our fitness or abilities. I probably never could have passed gym.

According to the Centers for Disease Control and Prevention, demonstrating an understanding of the benefits of physical activity, the appropriate use equipment, and performing self-assessments help to evaluate whether a student is learning in gym class.[49] This idea draws from the lifestyle physical activity goal concept. Grading in gym should be based on <u>what</u> you do

---

[49] The "Physical Education Curriculum Analysis Tool" published by the Centers for Disease Control and Prevention takes a comprehensive approach to assessment in physical education. It suggests that students be evaluated on knowledge as well as the ability to improve their individual performance.

not necessarily <u>how well</u> you do it. Fitness and skill-based testing take a different approach.

Fitness testing has a long history in physical education. [50] A national fitness test was instituted in the 1950s by American Association for Health, Physical Education and Recreation in response to reports suggesting that European children were more physically fit than American children. Since then, many different tests have been developed to evaluate physical fitness and motor skill. Wide use of fitness tests provide data that can be used to compare student performance to others of the same age and gender. The results can also be useful in shaping school policy regarding physical education.

As mentioned previously, a historical purpose of gym class was military service preparation for young men. Yet in the early 1940s, a large percentage of young men were disqualified from serving in the military—some because of physical fitness-related health issues. That does not necessarily mean that gym class was ineffective, but it does raise questions about the ability of a sports-oriented curriculum to improve physical fitness.

Tests are part of school, so testing often has a place in gym class. Some states require fitness testing for students. Where testing is not required, it is up to individual gym teachers to decide whether or not to test their students. Required testing provides data to evaluate students in relation to state or national standards. Results of non-required testing provide the teacher and the student with information that may be useful in helping the student succeed in gym class.

There is a difference between fitness tests and skill tests. Physical fitness tests evaluate the basic components of physical fitness strength, muscular endurance, cardiorespiratory fitness, and flexibility. Skill tests evaluate motor skill or movements related to sports like a softball throw, 100-yard dash, or a shuttle run. While fitness tests may be useful in gym class, a skill based test evaluates whether the student can do something as well as his/her peers.

---

[50] Keating and Silverman report on a study on the use of fitness tests in physical education.

Many of the people I interviewed were able to recall the components of fitness tests, but were not able to logically relate this to the activities in gym class. Others did not recall participating in any tests involving motor skills or sports skills. No one remembered developing an individual fitness plan based on the results. Fitness testing usually interrupted a series of team sporting activities which were resumed when the testing period concluded. Recent surveys indicate that many gym teachers take time to prepare students for fitness tests..[51] That would have been useful for Kendra, who says fitness testing made her mad since it always included activities that were not part of regular gym.

> When we did the President's Physical Fitness Test, we had to run and do all these things. Did they ever teach me to run? No. I was just supposed to miraculously know how to run or how to climb a freakin' rope. Of course I was the slowest person and I could not get up the rope. I guess they thought that we'd know how to that from the things we did in class. We didn't practice for that at all.

The result of fitness testing for Kendra was that it reinforced her poor physical self concept. I vaguely recall participating in skills tests like the softball throw and 100-yard dash in elementary school. But our gym teachers treated testing lightly. My personal experience with the President's Physical Fitness Test was sixth or seventh grade. I was new to the school. One day our gym teacher announced that we would spend several classes doing the test. She chose to do the hardest event first; if we failed to pass the Standing Broad Jump we were not allowed to participate in any further tests. According to my teacher, there was no point in wasting time administering tests to students who could not successfully complete all of the events. Those who could complete all of the events at a prescribed level were awarded a patch. The whole idea was kind of exciting to me. I had never done a Standing Broad Jump before and tried my best. Of course I fell short. I remember being very disappointed, and trying for weeks afterward at

---

[51] Pedagogy experts, teachers, school boards, and parents disagree about the amount of school time allocated to instruction and preparation for standardized tests. The activities used in fitness tests are often quite different from gym class activities. Preparation of students enables them to more effectively participate. See Silverman, Keating and Philips).

home to jump farther. I hoped I could change the teacher's mind and be allowed to participate in the remaining tests. Those of us who failed the tests were assigned the task of measuring and encouraging the girls who were still allowed to participate. The only thing I learned from this activity was that I lacked skill in another event in gym.

When fitness tests are used appropriately, they can be helpful to students and teachers. Theoretically students and teachers can work together to plan learning activities to address areas that need improvement. I have not actually met anyone who did this sort of thing in gym. When fitness tests are not used appropriately, it does leave a lasting negative impression..

Fitness tests do not measure exercise in terms of health or lifestyle. They do not capture whether a student is willing or able to exercise or be physically active outside of gym class. Students who perform better on fitness and skills tests are assumed to be more active than those who do not. Students who lack physical self-confidence are less likely to be active outside of gym class and probably do not perform as well on fitness tests.

George was aware that he lacked skill in gym class. He does not know how he was assigned to remedial gym in middle school. He does not recall a formal evaluation. He does suspect that his teacher knew he could benefit from additional help. Luckily the class helped him become "less pathetic" in gym. George's usual gym curriculum involved team sports. He spent time and effort trying to stay out of the way and not get hurt. Remedial gym introduced him to lifestyle oriented activities like weight training. That term he learned that how to improve his physical fitness.

> At first I felt like I was being stigmatized. But in the long run remedial gym was the best thing that could have been done for me. The teacher was nice. I never got good in gym, but I wasn't pathetic after that.

The progress George made in remedial gym might be captured on a fitness test. More important is how the class improved his physical self concept. Qualitative information like this may not be easily generalized to the larger

population. However, it is more memorable for the student than a score on a fitness test.

What students take away from gym class is important. That message has its roots in the curriculum and the instruction. A very small percentage of adults meet the national guidelines for physical activity. When students graduate from school, mandated fitness testing is left behind and for most students is forgotten. Students who did not succeed in gym remember the negative experiences. They remember wanting to try, but being unsuccessful at their attempts. Testing did not inspire them to try to succeed.

> They would give us a flexibility test where you had to touch your toes. My entire life, even as a child I could not touch my toes. I am not a flexible person. We would do this hop, skip and jump test every year from kindergarten to sixth grade. I never got it right. Nobody ever explained to me the difference between a hop and a jump. So I screwed it up every time.

Chapter 9

Costumes:

Perceptions of Gym Uniforms

I looked good in everything, but not in that gym suit.

Gym class uniforms are a time-honored tradition at many schools. Theoretically, wearing a uniform promotes discipline, teamwork, and structure in gym.[52] There is little evidence to back up these assumptions. A benefit of gym uniforms is that every student has the proper attire for exercise. What is different about gym uniforms is that they do not always look like "real clothes" that a person would wear for exercise. That makes a gym uniform feel like a costume.

The history of gym attire probably harkens back to the days when the purpose of gym was pre-military physical fitness preparation. Everyone dresses alike and moves in unison. The styles of gym costumes have changed over the years: from skirts to trousers to shorts. For women, gym uniforms were instrumental in making trousers a viable clothing option.[53] Erin was a student during this shift in fashion.

> When I was in elementary school, girls could not wear pants. So we got out there and played during recess in skirts and crinolines. Dressing out was important in high school gym class. We got to wear white t-shirts and shorts.

Erin does not recall her gym costume as attractive. Rather it served a utilitarian purpose. Being able to wear shorts and a t-shirt helped Erin to move

---

[52] A variety of opinions from students and teachers about gym uniforms are presented in "Should Students Be Required to Dress out in a Standard Uniform for Physical Education."

[53] Warner's book traces the history of women's fashions and the impact sports participation had on fashion trends. When women started having opportunities to exercise and play sports, the clothing options were not suited to the activities. Although skirts were the norm, women learned that it was much easier to play in pants or shorts.

more actively than the skirts she wore to school. Darren also wore a t-shirt and shorts for his junior high school the gym uniform.

> The boys' gym uniform clothes were really poorly fitting: baggy shorts and ill-fitting t-shirts and a jock strap. It is funny to me now because Abercrombie and Finch sells stuff that looks just 1970s gym clothes for an awful lot of money. It seems like every boy in Fire Island is wearing it now: a Seventies high school gym uniform.

Like Erin, Darren considered his gym costumes to be functional. But it did not make him feel good about gym because the outfit did not fit comfortably. Kendra's middle school gym uniform was uncomfortable for a different reason: it was revealing.

> Our junior high gym class uniforms were the worst. We wore a one-piece, zip up things that had navy blue shorts. The shorts were tight and not very long. The top was a blue and white horizontally striped sleeveless shell top that zipped up the back. It was unnecessarily revealing like something from the 1960s. A couple of the girls wore them backwards so they could be rebels and zip them up the front. The boys got to wear shorts and t-shirts, but we had these hideous outfits. None of the girls liked them.

Kendra was not comfortable with team sports in gym class and the uniform did nothing to make her feel better. It added to the feeling that she was awkward and exposed. Kelly's high school gym uniform was also unappealing.

> It was a one-piece, blue jumpsuit with shorts and a top that had horizontal stripes. It was ugly. It was not at all flattering.

Kelly was used to school uniforms. In elementary school she wore a wool uniform skirt and a white blouse to school every day. But she felt it was different from her gym suit in high school. She felt that her gym suit was also revealing. Jackie's gym suit was also a one-piece style.

> Our junior high gym uniforms were disgusting. It was sort of a salmon color. A one-piece outfit with shorts and a short-sleeve top that buttoned up the front. Usually you bought one from somebody who was graduating because nobody wanted to pay like a lot of money for those things.

The one-piece gym suit that Kendra, Kelly, and Jackie were required to wear sparks a vivid memory for any girl who had to wear one. They were shapeless, uncomfortable, and unattractive. The integrated top and shorts contributed to the strange manner in which it fit the body. Some of the earlier styles had bloomer shorts and were made of cotton that did not stretch or breathe. They were not comfortable and were anything but attractive. One of Barbara's classmates managed to modify her gym suit and make it fashionable.

> When I was in high school, everybody wore hip-hugger bellbottom pants. That was the style. There was a girl in my gym class that managed to take her little gym singlet and somehow turned it into some sort of hip-hugger thing. She just rolled it up and bunched it around so it became like short, hip-hugger shorts. She was like the sexiest thing alive in that outfit.

One piece outfits like the common style for girls' gym suits do not reflect any fashion trend for adolescent or young women in recent memory. At best these costumes resembled clothing designed for an infant or toddler. The gym suits were probably not initially designed to be stylish. Rather they were likely intended to create a class of amorphous, genderless individuals.

Being dressed properly for gym class is important from a safety standpoint. Clothing and inappropriate footwear can interfere with movement. When Francis was in middle school they did not change for gym. He wore regular clothing and street shoes to class because that was what he wore to school. Francis does not remember being very active in class. At Adam's middle school they specifically required white socks as a safety measure.

> For gym we had to buy the gym shorts, sneakers and white socks. They made a big deal about the white socks. You could never go to gym without white socks because if you got a blister and you got dye in your foot you'd get poisoned or something.

There are many arguments for and against requiring uniforms for physical education. Wilson notes that putting students into uniforms does not provide them

with the opportunity to make choices.[54] Samantha acknowledged that a benefit of uniforms at her school was that it put the rich and poor students into one group. Everybody looked similar which created an atmosphere of acceptance across socioeconomic groups. She noted that "everyone looked equally awful."

One of the things that many students do not like about gym class is changing their clothes.[55] The changing process takes time out of class. Changing clothes for gym promotes good personal hygiene, if the gym clothes are laundered. Jackie rarely remembered to wash her gym suit.

> We had gym class probably two or three times a week and you'd leave our salmon gym suits in a locker. They would get pretty ripe smelling by the end of the week. But nobody took them home and washed them in between classes.

The attire for Kelly's gym class in elementary school did not promote personal cleanliness either. That school did not have a gymnasium, locker rooms, or showers. Her recollection of changing for gym class may be familiar to other parochial school alumni.

> In elementary school we wore shorts under our wool uniform skirts for modestly. For gym, we pulled off our skirts and would wear our uniform blouses with our shorts. We all got to put on sneakers. That was a big deal because we were not allowed to wear sneakers to school.

Students who were not required to wear uniforms in gym did not seem to think of the gym class attire as a costume. At Kelly's school, the lack of formality to gym made it a relatively transition from academic classes to gym and back to the rest of her day. Barbara had a similar experience in elementary school, but middle school was different.

> When I was in grade school we used to have to change our shoes. But that was the only thing we had to change. Back then children all wore leather

---

[54] See "Should Students Be Required to Dress out in a Standard Uniform for Physical Education?" p. 12. Wilson's editorial raises the question as to whether teaching students how to dress for exercise and physical activity should be part of gym class curriculum.

[55] Activities like changing clothes and showering take time out of gym class. See Courtier, Chepko and Coughlin.

shoes with regular leather soles. In gym you had to wear tennis shoes, as they were called. We wore our regular clothes for gym and our tennis shoes. That was the only special thing. When we got to middle school, we actually had to wear these completely dorky little one-piece singlet things that were shorts and a top all together. These outfits were horrible. They were red, poorly made, and had been washed a billion times. They were thick cotton, one-size-fits-all, sack shaped to accommodate any person big or little. They were damned uncomfortable.

Dressing appropriately for exercise is important. That is something that students can and should learn. Safe exercise and physical activity requires proper clothing. Gym clothes should stretches to permit free movement, have few seams to minimize chafing, and be breathable to accommodate perspiration. Footwear must offer support for the whole foot and ankle and have the proper sole for the surface to encourage traction to reduce the risk of accidents.

But when the goal of gym is to promote regular exercise outside of class, it is important to note that lifestyle physical activity does not require a uniform. It does require empowerment for participants to make educated choices. Thus the singlets, bloomers, and jumpsuits that the girls wore did not resemble anything that most people would wear outside of class.

Nearly everyone I interviewed who was required to wear a uniform in gym remarked that the outfit was unattractive, uncomfortable, or both. Perhaps that is why dressing for class is sometimes counted as part the gym class grades. That gives some incentive for students to put on an unattractive and impractical outfit for class. Sensible costumes, like shorts and a t-shirt are more realistic options for students because they translate better to life outside of school.

A quick search of school requirements revealed that uniforms are still required for gym at some schools. Thankfully, the styles of gym uniforms for girls have changed over the years. Bloomers and jumpsuits for have given way to t-shirts and shorts, similar to the uniforms for boys. Students and gym teachers remain divided on whether gym uniforms are a good thing. It would make sense if the uniform managed to fulfill a curricular objective.

No one that I interviewed had fond memories for the girls' one-piece gym suit. I still recall feeling uncomfortable and cold in my powder-blue, jersey knit, striped-top gym suit. But dressing alike does inspire a feeling of camaraderie. Wearing an uncomfortable outfit that looked ridiculous did nothing to help me enjoy gym. From my vantage point in the bleachers I took solace in the fact that all the other girls looked equally silly.

It was like you had any choice. It was kind of leveling for the class. We were always equally dorky.

Chapter 10

Winners and Losers:

Feelings about Competition in Gym

I remember distinctly being told that sports were intended to teach you how to compete. That was its purpose. By constantly pressing the competitive part of it, it tended to make winners and losers out of kids in the class.

Healthy competition is a good thing. It is one of the things that students can learn to enjoy about gym. Being part of a team and working toward a collective goal can be fun, help broaden social networks, and teach teamwork fundamentals like cooperation. An emphasis on competition may interfere with those potential benefits. Many students need help to improve their motor skills and physical self-concept. An environment that provides encouragement is vital in gym class to help students attain that goal.[56] When the environment is focused on achievement it does not allow the students who lack skill—those who need the most help—to succeed.

The underlying etiquette for individual and team sports involves being gracious, ethical, and fair to all participants regardless of the score of the game. It is called sportsmanship. The process of learning team sports also introduces different social roles: leaders, followers, division of the group based on ability. Participants are expected to play well, encourage each other, and congratulate the winners, even if the winners are the opposing team. While doing something is important in gym, it may not necessarily translate into a perfect performance. In other words, achievement is not vital to the curriculum when the goal is mastery

---

[56] Students need positive reinforcement to help them be motivated to try in gym class. Presenting students with challenges can be motivating, but setting the proverbial bar too high can alienate students. See Alderman, Beighle and Pangrazi.

of motor skill or improved physical fitness. When a student improves motor skill or aspects of physical fitness, the student is a winner. This is not competition; it is a potential result of physical education. The student who does not improve motor skill or aspect of fitness is not a loser. Rather he/she is presented with an opportunity: to work on a plan for improvement in future terms. If educating students about physical activity and fitness is the goal of physical education, what is the purpose of competition in gym? Competition is appropriate in sports leagues, tournaments, inter-school athletics, and intramurals, not gym class.

When gym class aimed to improve physical fitness for future soldiers, competitive sports were seen as a method to achieve that goal. As the need for mass training of future able-bodied soldiers declined after World War II, and the rise in technology shifted the workforce away from physical labor toward occupations that were more sedentary. Thus there was a broad recognition of the health benefits of exercise. This gave physical education a shift in purpose which resulted in the need for an atmosphere of inclusiveness. Team sports still had a prominent role in gym, but the goal was physical fitness for all students.

This paradigm shift in physical education had additional contributory factors. Dr. Kenneth Cooper's book on aerobics and Richard Hittleman's book and television show on yoga introduced ideas of individual physical fitness to the mass market beginning in the 1960s. Alongside these trends was the rise in professional sports teams over the twentieth century. This created a polarization in the broader area of physical education. On one side was the general public who needed to understand physical fitness and create a personal fitness plan. On the other were elite athletes who undertook vigorous training and commanding hefty salaries to play competitive sports. Physical education students were trying to learn how to get fit but were playing—or watching—team sports in gym class.

The extensive use of team sports in gym is, perhaps, what confuses students and gym teachers alike; especially when the teachers are coaches of sports teams at school. Gym classes can serve as scouting and training grounds for

school sports teams. Marty remembers that several boys were picked in gym class and taught how to play basketball. These boys were the core group of basketball players at Marty's small town middle and high school. Adam had gym teachers who split time between coaching school sports and teaching gym. He recalls that some of the high school students were scouted for the sports teams by the coach/teachers. It was a big complement to be scouted in gym class.

Darren's gym teachers were also coaches. Their role in gym class was to coach the selected team sports activities in class. They did not teach the students about the health benefits of physical activity or how to create a personal fitness plan in gym class. Some of what he learned playing sports did carry over into his adult years. Darren had some team sports experiences in college and through his job.

> In college I did intramural soccer and softball. It was highly competitive but there was also a level of camaraderie because teams were organized around the dormitories and fraternities. Recently I was in London on business. Some of my colleagues organized some soccer scrimmages. I played and pretty much died after five minutes. I do not feel like it related to gym class. Gym was not something that most people wanted to do. There you were stuck with people you had no connection with. For awhile I played softball with a team at work. But now I am more interested in the ability to exercise and participate in an activity for health rather than in engaging in a competitive sports activity.

Intramural sports are a step down from interschool sports activities. They are generally considered to be more inclusive as they usually embrace students of a variety of skill levels. For many students who lack enough skill to make a varsity sports team, intramurals provide an opportunity for students to play sports. Winning was important in these competitions. But for Darren when the games were too competitive they lacked camaraderie. This prompted him to opt out rather than continue to play.

As previously discussed, it is not unusual for gym teachers to double up and teach other subjects in schools. Often this is a result of budgeting and policy related issues. But coaching sports for competitive play is quite different from

teaching about health and exercise. It probably feels natural for a coach to scout and recruit students in gym. Unfortunately this can lead toward an atmosphere of elitism. For Francis, gym class was a more alienating environment than marching band. When I asked him whether he thought marching band counted as exercise, he noted that they spent a lot of time marching with a high step. "That was exercise." His band met early in the morning every day before school to practice playing and marching. It was fun and not elitist like gym class was for him in middle school. He was exempt from gym in high school because he was in marching band. Francis felt that he learned to appreciate exercise in band, much more so than middle school gym. He compared his experience learning about music and to learning about exercise in gym class.

> Most people are capable of doing something. Suzuki's approach to violin playing makes it simple enough for anyone to try. It does not make a master, but enables the student to make music. Gym class should have done that, but it did not. Instead it was about achievement, winning, and elitism. The teachers expected every student to be the sports equivalent of a Rachmaninoff, or Einstein. Those who were not were left out. It was very black and white.

Tracy, who had trouble keeping up in gym because of her allergies and asthma, was also in marching band. It was not about getting physically fit, but marching helped her to lose weight and get in shape. Most of all it was fun. It required teamwork, but was not competitive. It was different from gym class. Kendra was also in marching band. It was also a friendly environment compared to gym class. In band she found the camaraderie and ability to enjoy movement.

> In marching band I wasn't a pariah. It was fun. But being outside and being with people and having to accomplish a group goal was fun. You could see from far away in the stands if people were out of line. It was really fun. It was a community and we were all working on the same thing.

> I think too we were all probably underdogs in other areas so we were very tolerant of people that were not so great at the physical stuff. While we had to march we did not have to have a perfect body or be incredibly coordinated. If we were out of line a step we would learn. It was not like you didn't hit the ball and then the whole team lost.

Marching band required participation from everyone. It was about working toward a collective accomplishment (i.e. teamwork). The competitive aspect of band centered about the audition and placement of the instrumentalists and auxiliary within their respective sections. Once students passed their auditions, the environment was centered about the common goal of making music and putting on a good show. The inclusive environment of band inspired positive memories for Tracy, Kendra, and Francis. It helped them to accomplish what they could not do in gym class: learn to appreciate movement and physical activity.

Adam learned that the purpose of sports was competition. When gym teachers get caught up in the idea of competition, students may marginalize themselves. For students who lack physical self confidence, winning a game may be perceived as an unattainable goal.

> The emphasis on winning made gym class different than summer camp which was physical activity pretty much all day. Camp was not very competitive as I recall, just educational and fun. It was a contrast. I had a great time at camp; it was not very competitive as I recall. It was mostly just educational and fun.

In many ways Adam felt that he learned more about exercising and being active at summer camp than he did in gym class. Both Francis and Adam learned about winners and losers in gym class. There was little room in between for the idea that anybody can be active and play a role on a sports team. Franco learned that losing in gym could result in punishments. The students on losing teams in activities like volleyball or basketball were required to do push-ups or run laps around the gym. This reinforced Franco's lack of interest in sports and competitive activities. Like Franco, Kelly viewed herself as non-competitive. She perceived a large gap between gym class and lifestyle physical activity.

> Girls did not play sports. We weren't concerned with fitness. We dieted if we wanted to lose weight. We skipped calories. We lived on celery and ice water. We didn't become active. Boys had sports not girls. Boys worked out. Fitness at home was a habit that was different from sports. My mother had always been active. It was not about winning anything. Just about being outside and moving to keep your body and mind busy. Exercising

your body was like exercising your mind by reading a book or doing a crossword puzzle.

For Kelly, and many other non-competitive students, sports involved aggressive behavior. Nucci and Young-Shim (2005) note that aggression may be cathartic, but it can also lead to further—inappropriate—aggressive behavior. Sportsmanship is a desirable attribute; aggression is not socially acceptable. Both are behaviors that can be learned by imitation and modeling in gym. That learning opportunity is dependent on the curriculum and the environment set by the gym teacher. Presenting students with appropriate challenges and teaching them skills in gym can help to motivate them in a positive environment. Significant challenges without proper instruction can encourage unacceptably aggressive behavior amongst students who simply want to win.

Gerald is a reserved, considerate, and thoughtful man. One of his more difficult memories of gym class involved wrestling. It was all about competing and winning.

> Wrestling was torture for me because I was so bad. I was so weak that they would have me wrestle against people that were in the weight class below me. At first they had me wrestling against guys in my weight class. It was no challenge for them; okay he's pinned. So then they had me wrestle against the weight class below me. I'm also not a very aggressive person. I think it was a combination of not being aggressive, not being strong, not wanting to hurt someone, and not wanting to hurt myself. So it was easier to just go along with it and get pinned.

George would let himself lose rather than try to compete. He did not learn any techniques to help him win in wrestling and he did not want to risk getting injured. Wrestling was about competition, not sport. He enjoyed and appreciated activities that were gentler like badminton, archery, and tetherball. To him wrestling was violent. It reinforced the notion that he was delicate and out of place among his peers in gym class.

Adam's experiences with wrestling left a significant mark. He remembers that he liked gym class until he was in seventh grade. Until that time they played

sports in an inclusive atmosphere. In seventh grade they had a unit on wrestling. Adam did not receive much instruction on how to wrestle. They just wrestled each other in win/lose matches.

> I didn't want to wrestle anybody. I didn't want to get hurt. I didn't want to hurt anybody. To me sports were about playing, not about pinning anybody or hurting anybody. Wrestling just looked like a way to hurt somebody or to get hurt. A lot of the kids in my class were some of the tougher ones and I didn't want get be caught on the mat. You had to be pinned to the mat by some hoodlum that was from my neighborhood.

> The whole class sat in a circle and every time two guys were called to the center it was like watching the Romans cheer on the lions to see who could get messed up the most. My name got called. I thought my opponent was really a tough kid, at least he always acted that way. He came running at me full speed and he hit my thighs, his feet kept running and I was just standing there. I realized that he was really not very strong. He couldn't get up enough steam to knock me over. Then I realized 'this was the guy I've been afraid of for two years?' So I picked him up and I just rolled him over and I landed on him and I held him down. Of course he was very upset because I was holding him down. I felt terrible because I felt like this is embarrassing for him. I thought I was finished.

> A few minutes later I get called a second time against a much tougher guy. The whistle goes off. He goes right at me but this time I dropped down and we were both kind of horizontal on the mat with him underneath. I realized that I wasn't strong enough to flip him. We stayed in that position with his head in my crotch for it seemed like a long time. What was probably three minutes felt like thirty. He kept trying to turn me and I just kept holding on. I won the match on points because I just held on.

Student's perceptions of gym class are important. If motor learning is an expected result of a carefully-crafted curriculum, wrestling did not help Adam or George accomplish much. Neither felt that they improved their skills or learned to appreciate movement.[57] Both of their impressions are about surviving the experience.

---

[57] None of the women I interviewed were required to wrestle in gym class. The men who participated in gym class wrestling were not able to describe their impressions about the physical fitness aspects of wrestling and why wrestling is included in gym class.

The experience of gym is subjective. Physical fitness is both subjective and objective. Components of physical fitness can be objectively measured, but appreciation for activity and sportsmanship are personal and thus more difficult to capture. When gym class is about winning or losing, nobody wins. Everybody loses something because it is not about learning.

> I think maybe gym teachers have a certain understanding of team sports dynamics that they're not passing on to the kids. We did not learn about sportsmanship in gym. In sports, I see players who can take a certain amount of ribbing in stride. It is either supportive or it serves to challenge the other player to do the best they can. Whereas to me it seems mean. It is something I never learned how to understand.

Chapter 11

Gang Showers, Puberty, and Rumors: Issues Surrounding Changing and Bathing at School

Gang showers, jock straps, and red rubber balls. That's what I remember most about gym.

Gym class conjures up different memories at various ages. The memories of elementary, middle, and high school revealed three distinct patterns, regardless of the separation of grades in school systems. Elementary school gym (from kindergarten through fifth or sixth grade) was recalled as non-competitive and enjoyable. Even when students were required to stand in lines and do calisthenics, it was viewed as informal, inclusive, and fun. All students were usually involved in games where the emphasis was on participation. In the middle/junior high school years (fifth or sixth grade through eighth), gym was more structured and became competitive. The primary activities were team sports such as basketball, volleyball, softball, and baseball. This is the age where elitism became an issue; where separation of sports-skilled and non-skilled students started to occur. Individual sports like wrestling and folk dance were introduced in middle school along with discussion of personal hygiene, sex, drugs, and health.

The atmosphere in gym class was different by middle school; it was no longer inclusive and often not fun. Exclusion and marginalization became a regular feature of class. Bullying and hazing occupied a prominent part of gym and were intertwined with socioeconomic status, sports skills, academic prowess, and sexual awareness. By high school (ninth through twelfth grade), gym was an obligation for many students. It was viewed as radically different from other required classes. While academic classes required work, gym involved showing

up, changing clothes, participating in a team sport, and getting dressed. The division between sports-skilled and non-skilled students was more pronounced. When skilled students were given more opportunity, non-skilled students were rarely penalized for lack of participation as long as they were dressed and in attendance.

The requirements to change clothing for gym and shower after class become a part of gym class in middle or high school. This coincides rather unfortunately with puberty and the early stages of sexual awareness. For many students the gym locker room was an uncomfortable place where they were vulnerable and exposed.

Dressing for gym is known to be a barrier for participation in gym. It takes time away from the amount of time scheduled for class. For elementary school students simply changing footwear can speed up the transition from academic courses to physical education. Gym is basically part of the day. Middle and high school get more complicated with uniforms, locker rooms, and showers. Gym has characteristics that are unlike any other class at school.

Students do not like being sweaty after class but they also do not like being required to shower after gym. It is an interesting paradox. The objections to showering usually involve time or the lack of privacy. Common shower rooms, also called "gang" showers make sense from an oversight perspective. When students can be observed they are less likely to have the opportunity to bully, haze, or engage in horseplay. Monitoring students in gym class can be tricky for gym teachers because students may feel violated if they feel watched. Many students feel uncomfortable in gang showers because they are modest, conscious of changes in their appearance, or are beginning to be aware of their sexuality.

Kelly was horrified at the prospect of showering in high school gym class. She describes herself as very modest. Although they had showers in the locker room, she was grateful that students were not required to shower after gym.

Freshman gym class we had to go and change into our gym suits in a
locker room. We were told that afterward we would have to take a
shower—in front of these other girls. I thought no way! We undressed
down to our bra and panties and then put on our gym suits. Luckily people
didn't make fun of each other or stare. Thankfully the shower thing was
never enforced.

Like Kelly, Barbara was very self conscious about changing clothes in
front of their classmates. For her, showering at school was out of the question.
Barbara recalls changing in middle school.

In middle school, we would go into a locker room and change our clothes
which was about the most traumatizing thing when I was twelve years old.
The teachers were sometimes in the locker room when we changed. It was
horrible. They wanted us to take showers after gym, but I managed to
avoid it. I usually was able to exploit a loophole in the teacher's attention
span.

The teacher was probably in the locker room at Barbara's school to keep
order. Sometimes the perception is that a gym teacher has other proclivities. The
image of masculine and lesbian female gym teachers is prevalent in movies.
George would not reveal details of rumors about the proclivities of a gym teacher
at his high school. The recollection made him uncomfortable and somewhat
fearful; like someone listening to a ghost story at a slumber party. For him the
memory was scary and enduring.

Kendra knew that boys were sometimes hazed in the gym locker rooms.
Perhaps that was why even though the locker rooms at her school had showers,
none of the girls showered after gym.

Our locker rooms had showers. We could have taken showers, but no one
ever forced the girls to do it. So no girls took showers. None of us. A male
friend of mine from junior high who is a teacher will not teach high
school. He will not teach kids older than a junior high school level because
he was so traumatized in high school. I don't know what happened to him.
But something happened in the locker room. It was not good. He will not
even talk about it.

The gym locker room put students in a potentially compromising position. They are in various stages of dress and undress. Anything valuable must be secured prior to joining class. Adam recalled that some of the boys in his gym class were aggressive. The locker room was ruled by the bullies at his school.

> It wasn't anything sexual. It was more about being shaken down for money. It was intimidation. We were vulnerable at that time. It was a pretty tough crowd in there. If you had money they thought it should be their money. I always found it advantageous to just get in and out of there in a hurry.

Darren's hall locker was near the gym. He witnessed a good amount of roughness in and around the gym locker room. Occasionally a boy would be thrown out in the hallway with no clothes on. Thankfully it never happened to him.

> The gym teacher's office was off of the locker room so there was probably somebody around looking. But I never perceived it as being supervised. It was sort of the cliché which you'd imagine: rowdy kids, who would rather not be there.

Encouraging good personal hygiene is an important aspect of health and exercise. health. At Jackie's high school, showers were required after gym class.

> Showering was generally a free for all. One time we took one girl's underclothes. Somehow or another they appeared in the Home-Ec freezer. Other things happened, but I was not involved. Luckily I was not the subject of any of the horseplay either.

The girls at her school were unsupervised in the locker room so showering was not about hygiene. Rather it was an opportunity for hazing and bullying. Jackie refers to it as horseplay, because in her mind the pranks were not harmful.

My first elementary school did not have a locker room or even a gym. We changed out of our school uniform skirts into shorts in the bathrooms or in the corners of the church basement. My first encounter with a locker room and showers occurred in fifth grade. In fifth grade I attended a public school where showers were required after gym. The gym teacher stood outside the locker room.

At the sound of any rowdy behavior, she would come into the locker room and restore order. About half of the girls took showers. I remember a few of the girls were very comfortable walking around naked. Like Barbara, Kelly, and Kendra, I was not comfortable undressing or showering in front of the other girls. I think one of my classmates told me that nobody could make me take a shower. I felt empowered to opt out. I gave myself a quick wipe down before dressing, ran a little water through the back of my hair, and waited to exit the locker room until it seemed like I had enough time to shower.

The gang shower seemed weird and I thought it was probably dirty if every student had to shower after gym. Somebody told me that most of the boys at our school had athlete's foot. That scared me so I checked my feet religiously all year for any signs. Miriam also thought locker rooms and gym showers were dirty places. She does not remember showering after gym class, but she did use the locker room for an experiment in science class.

> In science class we had to grow cultures. I got to go down to the boys' locker room and expose my Petrie dish to the air. Whatever was in the air would start growing on the dish. Boy did that culture grow. It was amazing!

The introduction of separate locker rooms added an aura of mystery to middle and high school for boys and girls. At Marty's high school, the only part of gym class that the girls talked about was that they received a grade for taking a shower after class.

> It was rumored at our high school that the girls were only graded on whether they took a shower. The teacher sat outside the shower and marked off the girls names when they came out. They didn't get graded on any activities just whether or not they took a shower.

The boys and girls at Marty's high school had separate gym. For some students gender segregation can be beneficial. Many girls become concerned with their physical appearance in middle school. This can interfere with their

willingness to participate in gym. Barbara recalled a girl from middle school who was obsessed with boys.

> My most vivid memory of gym involves this one girl. When we came into class, we would all have to line up in our lines. I always sat behind this girl. She was totally into boys. That was all she wanted was boys. Boys, boys, boys! She would sit right in front of me and I would think 'God will she ever stop thinking about boys?' There were not even any boys in our gym class, only girls—probably for good reason.

Barbara does not remember anything about the girl's sports skill or participation in gym. She only remembers that this girl spent her time in gym obsessing about boys and trying to make her gym suit look more attractive. Having co-ed gym class would probably have made it difficult for her classmate to concentrate.

Like Barbara, Erin's gym classes were separate for boys and girls in high school. For the girls getting their periods was a rite of passage as well as an excuse to opt out of gym class. Erin was angry at the girls who constantly sat out during class.

> Our gym outfits were embarrassing because we wore white shorts. Girls were maturing and getting their periods. Some of them would get ribbed because all of a sudden they had marking on the back of their white shorts. If the boys snuck into gym class, they would make fun of the girls.

> Back then when some girls were having a period the teacher encouraged them to sit out. They were excused to sit on the sidelines for a whole week. It was a badge of honor. It really irked me because our school was small and sometimes there were so many girls sitting out that we didn't have enough to play anything.

The girls tried to understand their menstrual cycle and how to hide it from the boys in school. On a certain level, having a period was embarrassing. On another level, it became an excuse to get out of class. Gym was the only class that would exempt a girl who had her period. Simone always tried to use it as an excuse to get out of gym. Kelly tried to use her period to opt out of gym at times, but her mother believed that exercise was important so it did not always work.

During puberty, adolescents are trying to understand their physical changes. Girls grow breasts and get their periods. They learn about bras, sanitary napkins, Midol, along with shaving their legs and underarms. While Erin was learning all of this, she found something curious about the boys' high school gym attire.

> I had never seen a jock strap before high school gym. After the boys had gym, I would look in to their locker room and see these jock straps all lined up. I would just look at them and try and figure out where they put them because I didn't really understand them at all.

Looking back on this it seemed very important to Erin at the time. As a girl, she wore a bra for breast support. She did not understand the male anatomy. Like many girls, she did not have older brothers or friends to tell her about athletic supporters. They were usually introduced to boys in middle school, often in sports or in gym class.

Adam learned about jock straps when he received a list of gym supplies for middle school. He does not remember anything on the list except for the athletic supporter. Adam was confused about needing support in gym.

> There was the whole conversation about wearing a jock strap. It was big doing that happened around seventh grade. They called it an athletic supporter. I didn't know what they were talking about. I remember coming home from school with a list of things I had to get for gym. I said to my mother I had to get an athletic supporter. I really thought it meant somebody who would cheer me on in gym. My mother and father explained it to me. When I put one on I didn't understand why it was any more protective than just underwear. It didn't seem to have any qualities that would prevent you from feeling agony if you got kicked there. But we were told you could never be in gym without it.

Gym class for Adam had safety rules: a jock strap and white socks. Just in case something bad happened. For boys the jock strap was a rite of passage, just like a training bra and regular bra were for girls. Introduction to the jock strap was probably easier for boys who had older brothers, or sensitive gym teachers.

Francis remembers being required to wear one beginning in middle school. He complied, but did not feel it would be helpful if he was hit.

The introduction of the jock strap was distressing for Darren. This was not because of the function of the jock strap. It was part of the gym uniform in middle school. The gym teacher frightened him.

> The most traumatic thing of all—I'm sure for most junior high school boys—was the jock strap. It was for me anyway. They introduced us to a jock strap. We had a really sadistic gym teacher who gave the lecture at the very beginning about the uniform. 'You must wear the uniform. You must wear the jock strap.' He's 'going to check to make sure you're wearing a jock strap.' He never said how he was going to check to see if you were wearing the jock strap. I don't even remember that he did actually check. But he certainly made it clear that he would. It was traumatic.

Darren was afraid that the gym teacher would actually check to see if he was wearing the jock strap. It was not clear whether the teacher would make him remove his shorts so he could see or would touch him to verify presence of an athletic supporter under his shorts. While Darren complied and wore his jock strap, he also was coming to terms with another part of his life.

> The difficult thing about junior high school in particular is that is when kids hit puberty. So you're discovering your sexuality. I was exploring and dealing with all of those emotions. I didn't know then that I was gay but I was experiencing something and not sure what it was. I went into a locker room and was thrown into this situation where for the first time you're seeing a lot of naked boys. It raises all sorts of confusing questions in your mind.

When Darren was in middle school and high school, being gay was not socially acceptable. He did not come out until he was an adult. His early sexual feelings were confusing because they were simultaneously erotic and taboo. The gym showers and locker room were a confusing place for him. A handsome and intelligent boy, Darren did not feel out of place anywhere else in school. He only felt awkward in the gym locker room.

Darren and Samuel were the only openly gay individuals that agreed to speak with me about gym class. Darren's gym class experience was difficult. He struggled with his preference and identity. At his schools, being homosexual was not acceptable.

Samuel's classes emphasized inclusion of all students regardless of sports skill or ability. He did not feel stigmatized because he was not interested in girls. Sexual preference was not perceived as a problem in Samuel's gym classes. As a contrast, Adam was heterosexual. He disliked wrestling in gym because of the homoerotic aspects of the activity.

> I hated every second of wrestling. I didn't want to be near these guys. I didn't want to be holding them. I didn't want them holding me and I didn't want their heads near my privates. I didn't want to be near theirs. I didn't like the grunting. I didn't like the smell. I didn't like the slipperiness of the other person. I didn't like anything about it. But there was no choice.

Adam's sexual preference was clear to him. But he also felt that there were overtones of homoeroticism in gym class, specifically when they participated in wrestling. This was an activity taught only to boys in gym. Like Gerald, Adam did not understand the educational purpose of wrestling.

Wrestling basically involves physically dominating someone and forcing them into submission. It is aggressive and purposed, involving strategy and strength. Girls did not wrestle in gym class. For boys who were required to wrestle, it involved intimate and sometimes sexual feelings.

The intersection of puberty, locker rooms, and group showers were uncomfortable for many of the people I interviewed. Rumors about sexual preference and possible deviances from social norms were common. Gym class took on a meaning that had little to do with exercise, sport, or physical activity. It was about finding one's physical and sexual place in live through physical self expression.

Chapter 12

Growing Up: How Gym Class Can Affect Adult Exercise and Physical Activity Participation

I hate exercise. I really hate exercise. All I need is for somebody to say 'oh let's don't do it' and I say 'okay, let's don't.'

Gym was unlike any other class because it involved physical competition, elitism, marginalization, bullying, and clothing changes. Gym rarely required homework, papers, or written tests. This combination created an environment that was difficult for many students to navigate. On a certain level, participating in gym was expected. Yet there were few repercussions for students who stood on the sidelines or could not meet fitness standards. Most of the people I asked perceived other "academic" classes to be more important than gym. They felt that they learned in other classes but not in gym. Gym was different.

The purpose of gym class was and remains unclear for many of the people I interviewed. Given the shifts in focus over the past fifty years, the confusion is warranted. Despite decades of recommendations from pedagogical experts to move away from team sports to a health-oriented curriculum, team sports have remained the primary vehicle for attempted learning. To students who did not develop adequate sports skills, team sports simply made no sense. They were unable to effectively participate and therefore they retreated or were banished to the sidelines. They were not marginalized in their other classes, even when those subjects had competitive activities. Many people perceived that the gym teacher did not care whether they were active or not. Somehow it was easy to be on the sidelines in gym.

Students like Samantha, Susan, and Eileen had different physical fitness and motor skill levels, but claim they did not learn much in gym. Samantha viewed gym as an inconvenience because it took time away from academics. As an adult, she stays active mowing the lawn, doing yard work, and playing with her children. Susan participated in after-school sports, but gym did little to help her physically condition. To her sports were cooperative, social, and inclusive—even though she had to pass a tryout to make the team. As an adult, Susan struggles with fitness, largely because she has little opportunity to play team sports. Eileen found away to be physically self expressive through dance and she became a professional dancer. She learned dance through lessons after school. Dance was not part of her gym class curriculum. None of them felt that gym class helped them to create a personal fitness plan or educated them about lifestyle physical activity.

Students like Franco and Clarisse learned to avoid activity. Gym was just something you had to get through in school. Franco would much rather drive a car than ride a bike or walk. He thinks mowing the lawn and shoveling snow are manual labor that should be avoided. By contrast Clarisse tries to be active. She goes to a fitness center a few times a week but will not try any activity that involves a ball. In many ways gym reinforced the notion for both of them that sports and gym are for other people.

Although he was made to run once in gym class as a punishment Frank discovered that he loved running and ran for years. He finds it amusing that the intended punishment backfired. Now he regularly practices yoga and Qi gong exercises, and sometimes walks or rides his bicycle for exercise. None of these are activities that he learned in gym class.

Samuel does not avoid activity, but he does not engage in planned exercise. He lives in an urban area so he remains active by walking. Even though his gym classes were inclusive, they were not instructional. The sports he played in gym were not important or significant for him. Like Frank, Kendra, and Tracy

he was in marching band. For him that represented meaningful activity. He never invested any importance in gym.

Erin expected high school gym to be important. She wanted to learn about sports. She really wanted to play basketball. Erin was sorely disappointed with high school gym.

> My mother had been on a girls' basketball team. She was a champion free-throw shooter. I was really excited that I would learn to play basketball in gym. But my school didn't have a girls' basketball team and I rarely got to play in gym. We would organize for sports but the teacher never taught us how to use our bodies effectively at all. We didn't warm up, stretch, or prepare. Since we usually played with just the right number for the sport, there was never another activity for the extra girls.

> My perception of gym was that it was different in other parts of the country. I thought that it was probably organized and they learned sports like basketball, volleyball, and tennis. I thought that because that was how I would see gym class portrayed in the movies. It was much more structured than my experience. It was the experience that I wanted but did not have.

Erin did not learn to play basketball in high school. She did not learn about physical fitness or the benefits of activity. She did learn about exercise and fitness from her college physical education teachers and from her parents.

> Our college gym instructors were in good shape, they modeled good behavior and good health habits. My mother did not exercise but she made healthy eating choices. My father was a farmer and a teacher. To do both of those things he pretty much had to keep moving. I have lived on a horse farm so I pitched and baled hay for years. Now I walk five days per week and try to swim laps at our pool. It's something—and something is better than nothing.

Living on a farm and learning about fitness from people other than her gym teacher helped Erin to lead an active life. At least she learned it somewhere but she did not achieve her dream of being on a basketball team. Neither did Marty. He opted out of high school gym because it looked rough. He folded towels instead. But he still tried to play basketball during the summer in his neighborhood.

On summer mornings I would wake up and listen for any sounds of basketballs bouncing at the basketball court near our house. When I heard someone playing I would jump out of bed, get dressed as quickly as I could, and go to the basketball court. There were kids of all ages and we would play all day.

Both Marty and Erin somehow learned that regular exercise and being physically active were important. They both learned that there were a variety of ways a person could be physically self-expressive in a way that could positively impact health. Neither felt that they learned this in gym class. Lifetime fitness skills were important things that they would have liked to learn more about in gym. Erin wished that she learned to play golf in gym class.

Golf would have been a lifetime thing that I could have done socially. I would have loved to have learned how to play golf in gym. I would've liked for us to have done exercises were not the calisthenics. Things like stretching, warming up, or things that I could have done at the office just sitting in a chair. That would have been useful.

Marty played pick-up basketball for about thirty years after high school. He also played tennis and as a high school counselor took a keen interest in physical education for students. He wanted to make sure that their gym class experience was better than his. Learning about lifestyle activity became very important to Marty as he grew older.

I had a heart attack and bypass surgery a few years ago. I was surprised that—instead of getting a disabled sticker to put on my car to park close— I was supposed to park far away and get the exercise walking. Now I usually don't take elevators unless it's going be quite a few stairs. I mow the yard for exercise and do a lot of snow shoveling in the winter. I also ride a stationary bike which is one of the most boring things in the world. I have my bike pointed toward the television set to get my mind off the pedaling.

Athletics and sports were not common activities for girls when Miriam was in school. Miriam took dance lessons as a child. She grew up to be a professional singer so she danced or took classes until she was in her forties. Miriam knew dance was beneficial to her but she did not view dance as exercise.

It something related to her occupation that was fun. Even though it was not her intention, dancing helped her to stay fit. Like many people I interviewed, she wished she had learned about the health benefits of exercise.

> I work with a personal trainer now. We work on making my muscles stronger around those areas of my body that are weak. It's so much easier to exercise when it's a social event. I enjoy working with her. I don't mind pushing myself or doing what she asks me to do because I know if she tells me to do it I'm going to be better. I really trust her. But I hate exercise.

> I wish I'd learned how valuable it would be to exercise and keep my body toned. Because I didn't, so I didn't. I just always assumed it would be there and then suddenly it wasn't. Maybe I would exercise if I had been taught as a young person. Few girls that I went to school with were remotely athletic. We didn't have any background in sports of any kind. When we get together and talk about it we just guffaw. We didn't have the things that the boys had and we didn't learn what the boys learned.

The gender differences in gym and physical activity seem to be more of an issue for women. The men who had separate gym class were aware that there were different resources allocated to them. Thankfully, girls now usually have better access to facilities and equipment now than they did prior to the trickle down effects of Title IX. Like many women in their forties, Jackie is trying to make up for what she did not learn. Although she thinks that her motor skills did not develop very well until after high school, she remembers that she was always active.

> The thing that's kind of mysterious to me now is that I was quite a tomboy actually. I liked to climb trees, train horses, play softball, and do all that sort of stuff. There was something about gym class that I did not enjoy. I guess I did not do well in a formalized setting doing sports that were not what I would choose to play.

> As part of physical education I wish I learned more about the rules of sports. In a business or corporate setting, the guys seem to know it. It's sort of innate for them; knowing what the rules are because they've been functioning in these rules systems since they were little kids. That's just not the norm for many women my age.

Jackie felt that training horses and playing with her brothers and cousins helped her physically develop much more than whatever she tried to do in gym class. Her active life outside of school helped to prepare her to be an active adult. Gym did not detract from her extracurricular activities. As an adult she is committed to walking in all kinds of weather; she walks to visit her patients and walks her dogs several times a day. Jackie did not learn about walking in fitness in gym class. She sometimes takes yoga and Pilates classes. All of her exercise and physical activity is independent. What she feels she missed most in gym was learning about teamwork.

The sports-centered education in Kendra's gym classes did not provide instruction about fitness, exercise and health. She did not feel that her classes were inclusive. Like Jackie, Kendra did not feel that she developed good motor skills in gym.

> My coordination kicked in during college—I took dance class. It was wonderful. The playing field was not level but it was less harsh than gym class. Everyone sort of understood that each person had value. You could excel or not and it really didn't matter. I don't think it was just about the teachers in college. A lot of the 'bun head' dancers would help you if you wanted them to. They wouldn't have picked on me because I was a better singer than dancer. I didn't pick on them for their singing.

> Maybe people choose to become gym teachers because they had a good experience in gym. But I wish my regular gym teachers had not been so passive. I wish they had been willing to help. When I could not tolerate the bullying, I pointed it out. I offered to do an activity by myself instead of playing volleyball. But I got no support. I got a D because I did not want to get picked on any more.

Dance and marching band provided Kendra with a meaningful way to learn about movement and being active. The sports that were the focus of gym class were not inclusive, cooperative, and physically expressive like dance. Dance was an activity that many people enjoyed in gym: social dance, folk dance, square dancing, line dancing, and aerobics. Although dance occupies a place in society as a performing art or social activity, rather than a sport, it is a physical activity.

Kelly loved dancing in gym class specifically because it was not competitive. Although Kelly says she does not like sports, as an adult she did learn to participate. She found that she enjoyed herself in situations that emphasized inclusion/fun rather than exclusion/competition.

> I finally learned how to play volleyball through one of my jobs. We had pickup games. Some guy decided to go out and take a bunch of sodas, a cooler and play a volleyball game. So on Wednesday nights we would get out there and somebody who knew something about the game said: 'here are the rules and positions. Here is what you do. Someone serves it, you bump, you set, you spike.' We rounded up other friends. Everybody brought someone. We kept it going for a couple of summers. Those were magical summers for me. It was the only time someone taught me. Someone finally explained it to me and I got it. I think that's why I have such a special place in my heart for volleyball.

> I wish that the emphasis in gym hadn't all been on team sports. I liked gym the most when I could do my own thing. It wasn't sports. It took me a long time to understand that fitness doesn't have to be about team sports. Some of us can be team players. But if we don't have the eye hand coordination or other athletic ability, we can still pursue fitness in our own way.

> Some friends that I worked with got me interested in swimming so I swam laps. Then they got me started running and then cycling. I did a few triathlons. I carried that on actually for about 5 years. I trained too hard, I hurt my knee, and I burned out. I hurt myself because I was always trying to run farther, faster, harder and I regret that.

> Then I realized I was facing forty and it became about; 'what kind of woman do I want to be as I grow into my middle years and older?' It was about feeling good and treating myself well and developing healthy self esteem. My attitude towards fitness and exercise has changed a lot in the last fifteen years. Now I walk several times a week and go to a women's boot camp twice per week.

When Kelly re-visited volleyball as an adult, there were people in the group who helped her to learn. The cooperative environment helped her to enjoy team sports for the first time. She also met other people who had not learned the rules or skills of sports in gym class. That comforted her and helped her self-

esteem. It helped her to be confident enough to try other individual sports and learn how to compete.

George learned how to compete, but not in gym. Being active on a recreational basis was quite different from gym. His experience in remedial gym was more applicable to lifestyle than his usual sports-based classes.

> Remedial gym was probably the best thing that happened for me. The class was small, I made friends, and I learned to lift weights. It wasn't at all like regular gym. My memories of regular gym are almost all negative. Running and wrestling in gym were torture. I hated—and was scared of—football. I was so afraid of getting tackled. I hated getting picked last if my cousin wasn't the captain. I got the wind knocked out of me playing soccer. It scared me away from doing that sort of stuff even more.

> I loved bike riding. I was as good as anyone else in bike riding. I used to go bowling and play tennis. But I am not real tough. I'm not good at things where I have to try to take advantage of someone else. When I used to do business deals I'd always want to make sure it was fair to the other side which is good but it's not tough enough. I'm not an aggressive person. That has its advantages and disadvantages. In math and chess clubs I would hope to win but it didn't matter. It was more about competing against myself and trying to get it right. Gym involved a different type of competition.

The delicate balance between competition and aggression was difficult for sensitive students like George who lacked sports skill. Adam had skill, and he enjoyed competing. But he felt that aggressive behavior detracted from his ability to participate in gym. Adam felt like he lost something of himself during wrestling in gym class.

> I felt really bad after wrestling in seventh grade because one of the kids that I wrestled—and beat—died suddenly in high school. I felt terrible about his death. Nothing I had done was related to it or caused it. It was just the idea that somebody had died and I had been the person who had wrestled him to the ground and held him down at some point in his life. I didn't feel at all good about that. All I remember about this kid is that I was shoving him around a mat and holding him down. That probably wasn't a very pleasant part of his existence. I really did not want to be part of something where I am hurting somebody and that's how they would remember me.

He connected wrestling with relationships. Adam was not deliberately demeaning to his classmate, yet wrestling made him feel bad. He was competing and doing what he was instructed to do. Adam did not learn specific skills or improve his fitness through wrestling in gym.

He exercises regularly now and feels that daily exercise benefits his health. He usually walks to work, cycles several times each week, and lifts weights occasionally. Walking, biking, and strength training were not part of his gym class curriculum.

> Almost all of the physical education that I received was game oriented. It was all learning how to play a sport. The kids who were highly skilled dominated the game. Then it was no fun. When I got out of college I played a lot of soccer and cycled because I lived in Europe. Then I moved back to the U.S. and team sports were not convenient. I realized that in order to maintain a good exercise routine, it had to be part of my daily routine. It also had to be convenient. In other words, if I had to drive to go do something in bad weather I would probably skip it.

> I feel better when I exercise. I feel more relaxed, healthy, I think more clearly, and I sleep better. I've got no pain which is unusual for someone my age. When I do a long bike ride I work out both my mind and body because I think through things and enjoy the scenery.

Given Adam's athletic abilities and interest in sports, it was unusual that he did not have a good experience in gym class. His perspective about gym, competition, sports, and lifestyle is interesting. He does see them as inter-related issues but he has separated them in his mind. Exercising and being active are part of his life; team sports and competition is something from the past. Over the years he learned to be physically active because it feels good. That lesson did not come from gym; ultimately he was self-taught.

Barbara feels that she is active out of necessity. When she exercises, she tries to find activities that she can enjoy. She still does not feel that she would join a team activity if the opportunity arose.

> I try not to do things that I don't enjoy. Right now I go to the gym about four days a week and I ride the stationary bike and I read for thirty to fifty

minutes. I ride my bike outside in the summer. I walk a great deal, not for fitness, but because I don't have my car during the day. Sometimes I walk as an activity for an afternoon. It's not about the walking. It's about the grandeur of the city and seeing stuff I've never seen, I rarely notice I've walked six or eight miles.

I wish I had learned how to participate in a group sport without it being quite so daunting. I wish that they could have taught me what the point of the group sport was and that they could have made it an atmosphere of acceptable inclusiveness. I wish I could have learned how to function within a team in a way that I didn't feel was threatening.

Darren did learn how to play on a sports team. He learned the skills that students like Jackie, Miriam, and Barbara did not learn. Darren learned about individual sports. But he views fitness as an adult to be quite different from what he learned in gym.

You think about the gym class and what going to a gym as an adult means. They are so completely different. There's nothing about going to a gym as an adult that was anything like what I learned in school. Weight training and cardio is how I perceive fitness today but they are not what I was taught in gym. How fit you are as a child is important and I'm sure to some extent helps you later on in life. But the way children become and stay fit is not the same as the way adults approach fitness.

I wish they taught us about time management. For kids that is probably not an issue, but it is certainly one of the barriers I face. Maybe I'm not prioritizing fitness as high as I should. But I take the stairs most of the time and I walk instead of taking cabs. I don't think gym class did much to prepare me for exercise as an adult.

Quantitative research has consistently found that most adults do not exercise regularly. Based on qualitative experiences of physical education amongst the people that I interviewed, it is easy to understand why. People don't know what to do. Many students did not learn how to exercise in gym. Team sports opportunities are not plentiful for most adults, and for many of them it is not a desirable activity. When opportunities do exist, students who did not master the skills,or learn how to be part of a team, are not likely to join a league. There

would be little point if they were showing up at a game to sit on the sidelines and watch others play.

The purpose of this book is not to chastise gym teachers, but to look at a system that has not satisfactorily accomplished the mission of physically educating students. The subjects in this book range in age from eighteen to sixty four. Their experiences in K-12 gym class spread over years in which there were shifts in curriculum and instruction for physical education. Many gym teachers try their best to meet state and national standards by using the resources and training available to them. But as Kendra noted, they probably became gym teachers because they did well in gym. It was familiar territory so they knew what to do and how to help that carry over into life outside of school.

Enjoyment is important in gym. Class is difficult for students who do not feel that they can make a contribution to the team. It is difficult when students do not know how to play. The typical set up for gym class does not lend itself well to teaching individual sports and lifestyle activities. The adult work and life schedule is not conducive to daily team sports participation. It is an interesting paradox.

Most of the people I interviewed did not find gym class to be fun or useful. I kept hoping to meet a success story. Gym was either a non-issue or a difficult experience for many people. Even some skilled students like Eileen and Adam did not see value in gym, unlike my graduate school classmates who enjoyed gym class. They felt that they learned about and played a variety of sports. Gym helped them develop positive physical self-perception, acquire skills, and learn about teamwork. They picked the teams and played while others—like me—sat on the sidelines. Playing was probably not painful, but watching did nothing to help students learn what was expected. Ultimately, everyone learned something about school, life, or themselves.

In the end, Marty earned his A for folding towels in gym but not doing anything physical. Miriam never did learn to play pool well, but Erin became quite skilled at poker. Gerald benefitted greatly from remedial gym. Barbara

never did learn how to hit a softball and still fears team sports. Kelly learned to exercise after college, but she remembers the names of the bullies from gym. Tracy walked and jogged a ten mile race just to see if she could do it. But she carries with her the baggage of a little girl who could not keep up.

My friend Amy recently reminded me that I was "an incredibly uncoordinated child." She was right. Gym class did not help me improve my motor skills. I never developed good eye-hand coordination. I have difficulty catching and hitting a ball. In gym I basically learned to stay out of the way, even when I wanted to play. But I eventually learned about fitness and activity. My first dance teacher helped me to appreciate movement. Learning to lift weights helped me feel empowered. Taking yoga and Pilates classes helped me feel aligned and centered. I taught myself to run. I remember running my first mile non-stop. I was thirty-three years old. Running helped me feel free. It is a shame I waited so long because it was exhilarating. I wish I had learned how to physically condition for running in gym class.

Much of what is learned in elementary, middle school, and high school prepared students for some aspect of life. I met people who failed other courses in school but I did not meet anyone else who failed gym. Since I have gone on to become a fitness professional that probably makes me some kind of success story. It did give me empathy and make me want to try harder. In some ways I think I succeeded despite gym class. Since I was not skilled at sports, I was forced to seek out individual and lifestyle-oriented activities. Ultimately that prepared me for the transition to adulthood. Like Darren and many other adults, I have struggled with time management. I have not always been successful in maintaining a fitness routine, but I know what I need to do. I did not learn that until after college.

Educating adults about exercise and fitness is very rewarding. Listening to their recollections of gym class was funny, sad, and confusing. The stories here are powerful. They shed light on why people who may have had similar

experiences do not exercise regularly. Many do not because they do not know how to exercise; gym did not physically educate them. Their thoughts and recollections cannot answer everything because their experiences are personal. Although they may have passed gym class, gym class ultimately failed them.

Bibliography

"About the Council: President's Council Overview". Washington, DC. (August 2, 2009): The President's Council on Physical Fitness and Sports, Department of Health and Human Services. August 2 2009. <http://www.fitness.gov/about_overview.htm>.

Alderman, Brandon L., Aaron Beighle, and Robert P. Pangrazi. "Enhancing Motivation in Physical Education." JOPERD 77.2 (2006): 41-51.

Aluede, Oyaziwo, et al. "A Review of the Extent, Nature, Characteristics and Effects of Bullying Behaviour in Schools." J of Instruct Psych 35.2 (2008): 151-58.

Amade-Escot, Chantal, and Christine Amans-Passaga. "Quality Physical Education: A Review from Situated Research (1995-2005)." Int J Phys Educ 43.4 (2006): 162-72.

---. "Quality Physical Education: A Review from Situated Research (1995-2005); Part Two: "Teacher Education" And "Student Learning"." Int J Phys Educ 44 (2007): 4-11.

Anderssen, Norman. "Perception of Physical Education Classes among Young Adolescents: Do Physical Education Classes Provide Equal Opportunities to All Students?" Health Educ Res 8.2 (1993): 167-79.

Bailey, Richard. "Evaluating the Relationship between Physical Education, Sport and Social Inclusion." Educ Rev 57 (2005): 71-90.

---. "Physical Education and Sport in Schools: A Review of Benefits and Outcomes." J Sch Health 76.8 (2006): 397-401.

Barney, David, and Brad Strand. "Do High School Students Know What Practices Are Appropriate in Physical Education." High Sch J 92.1 (2008): 33-40.

Barrett, Kate R. "Learning to Move - Moving to Learn: Discussion at the Crossroads." Theory into Practice 12.2 (1973): 109-19.

Beaty, Lee A., and Erick B. Alexeyev. "The Problem of School Bullies: What the Research Tells Us." Adolesc 43.169 (2008): 1-11.

Boiche, Julie C. S., et al. "Students' Motivational Profiles and Achievement Outcomes in Physical Education: A Self-Determination Perspective." J Educ Psych 100.3 (2008): 688-701.

Borer, Katarina T. Exercise Endocrinology. 2nd ed. Champaign, IL: Human Kinetics, 2003.

Camp, Frederick S. "Physical Education and Military Drill: What Should Be Our Policy?: A Superintendent's Report." Sch Rev 25.8 (1917): 537-45.

Caspersen, Carl J., Kenneth E. Powell, and Gregory M. Christenson. "Physical Activity, Exercise, and Physical Fitness: Definitions and Distinctions for Health-Related Research." Pub Health Rep 100.2 (1985): 126-31.

Cawley, J., C. Meyerhoefer, and D. Newhouse. "Not Your Father's P.E.: Obesity, Exercise, and the Role of the Schools." Education Next 6.4 (2006): 60-66.

Cawley, John, Chad Meyerhoefer, and David Newhouse. "Not Your Father's Pe: Obesity, Exercise, and the Role of Schools." Educ Next 6.4 (2006): 60-66.

Choi, Hoon-Seok, and John M. Levine. "Minority Influence in Work Teams: The Impact of Newcomers." J of Exper Soc Psych 40.2 (2004): 273-81.

Comprehensive Health Education and Physical Education Curriculum Framework. Trenton, NJ: New Jersey Department of Education, 1999.

Constantinou, Phoebe, Mara Manson, and Stephen Silverman. "Female Students' Perceptions About Gender-Role Stereotypes and Their Influence on Attitude toward Physical Education." Phys Educ 66.2 (2009): 85-96.

Couturier, Lynn E., Steveda Chepko, and Mary Ann Coughlin. "Student Voices-- What Middle and High School Students Have to Say About Physical Education." Phys Educ 62.4 (2005): 170-77.

---. "Whose Gym Is It? Gendered Perspectives on Middle and Secondary School Physical Education." Phys Educ 64.3 (2007): 152-58.

Cowley, W.H. "Challenge to Physical Education." J Higher Ed 16.4 (1945): 175-77.

DeWitt, R. T. "War and the Philosophy of Physical Education." Peabody J Educ 20.1 (1942): 23-28.

Erwin, Heather E., and Darla M. Castelli. "National Physical Education Standards: A Summary of Student Performance and Its Correlates." Res Q Exerc Sport 79.4 (2008): 495-505.

"The Federal Government Takes on Physical Fitness". Boston, MA. Historical Resources. John F. Kennedy Presidential Library and Museum. August 2 2009. <http://www.jfklibrary.org/Historical+Resources/JFK+in+History/The+Federal+Government+Takes+on+Physical+Fitness+Page+3.htm>.

Fraser-Thomas, J.L., and C. Beaudoin. "Implementing a Physical Education Curriculum: Two Teachers' Experiences." Can J Ed 2.3 (2002): 249-68.

Gini, G., and T. Pozzoli. "Association between Bullying and Psychosomatic Problems: A Meta-Analysis." Pediatrics 123.3 (2009): 1059-65.

Gutierrez, Melchor, and Luis Miguel Ruiz. "Perceived Motivational Climate, Sportsmanship, and Students' Attitudes toward Physical Education Classes and Teachers." Percept Mot Skills 108.1 (2009): 308-26.

Hardin, Brent. "Physical Education Teachers' Reflections on Preparation for Inclusion." Phys Educ 62 (2005): 44-56.

"Issues: Should Students Be Required to Dress out in a Standard Uniform for Physical Education?" JOPERD 76.4 (2005): 12-15.

Jankauskiene, Rasa, et al. "Associations between School Bullying and Psychosocial Factors." Soc Behav & Personality 36.2 (2008): 145-61.

Keating, Xiaofen Deng, and Stephen Silverman. "Teachers' Use of Fitness Tests in School-Based Physical Education Programs." Meas Phys Educ Exer Sci 8.3 (2004): 145-65.

Lund, Jacalyn, et al. "Professional Dispositions: What Are We Teaching Prospective Physical Education Teachers?" Phys Educ 64 (2007): 38-47.

MacDougall, Colin, Wendy Schiller, and Philip Darbyshire. "We Have to Live in the Future." Early Child Dev and Care 174 (2004): 369-87.

MacPhail, Ann, et al. "Children's Experiences of Fun and Enjoyment During a Season of Sport Education." Res Q Exerc Sport 79.7 (2008): 344-55.

McCullick, Bryan, et al. "Butches, Bullies and Buffoons: Images of Physical Education Teachers in the Movies." Sport, Educ and Soc 8.1 (2003): 3-16.

McLoughlin, William. "Understanding How Schools Fail Children." Int Rev of Educ 29 (1983): 59-72.

Menesini, Ersilia, Marco Modena, and Franca Tani. "Bullying and Victimization in Adolescence: Concurrent and Stable Roles and Psychological Health Symptoms." J Genet Psychol 170.2 (2009): 115-33.

Mood, Dale P., Allen W. Jackson, and James R. Morrow, Jr. "Measurement of Physical Fitness and Physical Activity: Fifty Years of Change." Meas Phys Ed Exer Sci 11.4 (2007): 217-27.

Morgan, Philip. "Teacher Perceptions of Physical Education in the Primary School: Attitudes, Values and Curriculum Preferences." Phys Educ 65.1 (2008): 46-56.

Morrow, James R., Jr., et al. "1958-2008: 50 Years of Youth Fitness Tests in the United States.(Special Topic)(Clinical Report)." Res Q Exerc Sport 80.1 (2009): 1(11).

"National Standards for Physical Education". Reston, VA. National Association for Sport and Physical Education. August 2 2009. <http://www.aahperd.org/Naspe/template.cfm?template=publications-nationalstandards.html>.

Nucci, Christine, and Kim Young-Shim. "Improving Socialization through Sport: An Analytic Review of Literature on Aggression and Sportsmanship." Phys Educ 62.3 (2005): 123-9.

Phillips, Amber. "A Comparison of National Board Certified Teachers with Non-National Board Certified Teachers on Student Competency in High School Physical Education." Phys Educ 65.3 (2008): 114-21.

Physical Activity and Health: A Report of the Surgeon General. Atlanta, GA: U.S. Department of Health and Human Services, Centers for Disease Control and Prevention, National Center for Chronic Disease Prevention and Health Promotion, 1996.

"Physical Education Curriculum Analysis Tool." Ed. Department of Health and Human Services. Atlanta, GA, 2006.

Ridgers, Nicola D, Delia M.A. Fazey, and Stuart J. Fairclught. "Perceptions of Athletic Competence and Fear of Negative Evaluation During Physical Education." Br J Educ Psychol 77.2 (2007): 339-49.

Sawyer, Thomas H. "Point-Counterpoint: The Physically Illiterate Physical
    Educator." Phys Educ 63.1 (1996): 2-7.
Shephard, Roy J., and Francois Trudeau. "Research on the Outcomes of
    Elementary School Physical Education." Elem Sch J 108.3 (2008): 251-
    64.
Silverman, Stephen J., Pamela Hodges Kulinna, and Gary Crull. "Skill-Related
    Task Structures, Explicitness, and Accountability: Relationships with
    Student Achievement." Res Q Exerc Sport 66 (1995): 32-40.
Silverman, Stephen, Xiaofen Deng Keating, and Sharon R. Phillips. "A Lasting
    Impression: A Pedagogical Perspective on Youth Fitness Testing." Meas
    Phys Ed Exer Sci 12.3 (2008): 146-66.
Solmon, Melinda A., and Jo A. Carter. "Kindergarten and First-Grade Students'
    Perceptions of Physical Education in One Teacher's Classes." Elem Sch J
    96.4 (1995): 355-65.
Totura, Christine M. Wienke, et al. "Multiple Informants in the Assessment of
    Psychological, Behavioral, and Academic Correlates of Bullying and
    Victimization in Middle School." J Adolesc 32.2 (2009): 193-211.
Treanor, Laura, and Lynn Housner. "Shaping up Physical Education." Educ Dig
    64.9 (1999): 58-61.
Tripp, April, Terry L. Rizzo, and Linda Webbert. "Inclusion in Physical
    Education: Changing the Culture." JOPERD 78.2 (2007): 3237.
Trouillard, David, et al. "Relation between Teachers' Early Expectations and
    Students' Later Perceived Competence in Physical Education Classes:
    Autonomy-Supportive Climate as a Moderator. Journal of Educational
    Psychology, 98(1), 75-86." J Educ Psych 98 (2006): 75-86.
Warner, Patricia Campbell. When the Girls Came out to Play: The Birth of
    American Sportswear. University of Massachusetts, 2006.
Welk, Gregory J, and Jodee A Schaben. "Psychosocial Correlates of Physical
    Activity in Children: A Study of Relationships When Children Have
    Similar Opportunities to Be Active." Meas Phys Ed Exer Sci 8.2 (2004):
    63-81.
Williams, Jesse. "Physical Education in the School." Sch Rev 34.4 (1926): 285-
    94.
Williams, Neil F., and Jenna Germain. "Fitness in Disguise: Fitness Activities
    Can Actually Be Enjoyed Rather Than Endured." JOPERD 79.7 (2008):
    35-56.
Xiang, Ping, Ron E. McBride, and Melinda A. Solmon. "Motivational Climates in
    Ten Teachers' Elementary Physical Education Classes: An Achievement
    Goal Theory Approach." Elem Sch J 104.1 (2003): 71-91.

Index

Virginia S. Cowen

Dr. Virginia S. Cowen is Assistant Professor of Massage Therapy in the Department of Health, Physical Education, and Dance at Queensborough Community College, the City University of New York (CUNY) in Bayside, New York. Dr. Cowen received her Ph.D. in Exercise and Wellness from Arizona State University.